*Sky Burial*

Random House Canada

# Sky Burial

AN EPIC LOVE STORY OF TIBET

XINRAN

*Translated from the Chinese by*
*Julia Lovell and Esther Tyldesley*

Originally published in Great Britain in 2004 by Chatto & Windus.

www.randomhouse.ca

Random House Canada and colophon are trademarks

Library and Archives Canada Cataloguing in Publication

Xinran, 1958–
  Sky burial

ISBN 0-679-31360-5

1. Wen, Shu. 2. Tibet (China)—Social life and customs—20th century. 3. Tibet (China)—History—1951–. 4. Tibet (China)—Biography. I. Title.

DS786.X55 2005     951'.505'092    C2004-905728-6

Printed and bound in the United States of America

1  2  3  4  5  6  7  8  9  10

*For Toby*

*who knows how to share*
*love and experience*
*space and silence*

This version of *Sky Burial* differs slightly from the Chinese original. During the translation process, the author worked with her translators and editor to make sure that all elements of the book were accessible to non-Chinese readers.

In Chinese names, the surname is placed before the first name. Shu Wen's first name is therefore Wen.

In 1994 I was working as a journalist in Nanjing. During the week, I presented a nightly radio program that discussed various aspects of Chinese women's lives. One of my listeners called me from Suzhou to say that he had met a strange woman in the street. They had both been buying rice soup from a street vendor and had started talking. The woman had just come back from Tibet. He thought that I might find it interesting to interview her. She was called Shu Wen. He gave me the name of the small hotel where she was staying.

My curiosity awakened, I made the four-hour bus journey from Nanjing to the busy town of Suzhou, which despite modern redevelopment still retains its beauty—its canals, its pretty courtyard houses with their moon gates and decorated eaves, its water gardens, and its ancient tradition of silk making. There, in a teahouse belonging to the small hotel next door, I found an old woman dressed in Tibetan clothing, smelling strongly of old leather, rancid milk, and animal dung. Her gray hair hung in two untidy plaits and her skin was lined and weather-beaten. Yet, although she seemed so Tibetan, she had the facial characteristics of a Chinese woman—a small, slightly snub nose, an "apricot mouth." When she began to speak, her accent immediately confirmed to me that she was indeed Chinese. What, then, explained her Tibetan appearance?

For two days, I listened to her story. When I returned to Nanjing my head was reeling. I realized that I had just met one of the most exceptional women I would ever know.

I never saw her again, but her story did not leave my mind, so finally I felt I must share it with others.

*Sky Burial*

1

*Shu Wen*


Her inscrutable eyes looked past me at the world outside the window—the crowded street, the noisy traffic, the regimented lines of modern tower blocks. What could she see there that held such interest? I tried to draw her attention back.

"How long were you in Tibet?"

"More than thirty years," she said softly.

"Thirty years! But why did you go there? For what?"

"For love," she answered simply, again looking far beyond me at the empty sky outside.

"For love?"

"My husband was a doctor in the People's Liberation Army. His unit was sent to Tibet. Two months later, I received notification that he had been lost in action. We had been married for less than a hundred days.

"I refused to accept that he was dead," she continued. "No one at the military headquarters could tell me anything about how he had died. The only thing I could think of was to go to Tibet myself and find him."

I stared at her in disbelief. I could not imagine how a young woman at that time could have dreamed of traveling to a place as distant and as terrifying as Tibet. I myself had been on a short journalistic assignment to the eastern edge of Tibet in 1984. I had been overwhelmed by the altitude, the empty awe-inspiring landscape, and the harsh living conditions.

"I was a young woman in love," she said. "I did not think about what I might be facing. I just wanted to find my husband."

I had heard many love stories from callers to my radio program, but never one like this. My listeners were used to a society where it was traditional to suppress emotions and hide one's thoughts. I had not imagined that the young people of my mother's generation could love each other so passionately. People did not talk much about that time, still less about the bloody conflict between the Tibetans and the Chinese. I yearned to know this woman's story, which came from a time when China was recovering from the previous decade's devastating civil war between the Nationalists and Communists, and Mao was rebuilding the motherland.

"How did you meet your husband?"

"In Nanjing," she replied, her eyes softening slightly. "I was born there. Kejun and I met at medical school."

That morning, Shu Wen told me about her youth. She spoke like a woman who was unused to conversation, pausing often and gazing into the distance. But even after all this time, her words burned with love for her husband.

"I was seventeen when the Communists took control of the whole country in 1949. I remember being swept up in the wave of optimism that was flooding China. My father worked as a clerk in a Western company. He hadn't been to school, but he had taught himself. He believed strongly that my sister and I should receive an education. We were very lucky. Most of the population at this time were illiterate peasants. I went to a missionary school and then to Jingling Girls College to study medicine. The school had been started by an American woman in 1915. At that time there were only five Chinese students. When I was there, there were more than one hundred. After two years, I was able to go to the university to study medicine. I chose to specialize in dermatology.

"Kejun and I met when he was twenty-five and I was twenty-two. When I first saw him, he was acting as a laboratory assistant to the teacher in a dissection class. I had never seen a human being cut up before. I hid like a frightened animal behind my classmates, too nervous even to look at the white corpse soaked in formalin. Kejun kept catching my eye and smiling. He seemed to understand and sympathize with me. Later that day, he came looking for me. He loaned me a book of colored anatomy diagrams. He told me that I would conquer my fear if I studied them first. He was right. After reading the book several times over, I found the next dissection class much easier. From then on, Kejun patiently answered all my questions. Soon he became more than a big brother or a teacher to me. I began to love him with all my heart."

Shu Wen's eyes were so still—locked on something I couldn't see.

"Everybody admired Kejun," she continued. "He had lost all his relatives during the Sino-Japanese War, and the government had paid for him to go to medical school. Because he was determined to repay this debt, he worked hard and was an outstanding student. But he was also kind and gentle to everyone around him, particularly to me. I was so happy . . . Then Kejun's professor came back from a visit to the battlefields of the Korean War and told Kejun of how the brave soldiers who were hurt and crippled in those terrible battles had to do without doctors and medicine, how nine out of ten of them died. The professor said he would have stayed there to help if he hadn't thought it his responsibility to pass on his medical knowledge to a new generation, so that more hospitals could have trained surgical staff. In war, medicine was the only lifeline: whatever the rights and wrongs of combat, saving the dying and helping the wounded were heroic acts.

"Kejun was deeply impressed by what his mentor had told him. He talked to me about it. The army was in desperate need of surgeons to help its wounded. He felt he ought to join up. Although I was frightened for him, I didn't want to hold him back. We were all suffering hardship at that time, but we knew it was for the greater good of the country. Everything was changing in China. Many people were packing their bags and heading for poor rural areas to carry out land reform, or going to the barren, uninhabited borderlands to turn the wilderness into fields. They went to the northeast and northwest to look for oil, or deep into the mountains and forests to fell trees and build railways. We regarded separation from our loved ones as a chance to demonstrate our loyalty to the motherland."

SHU WEN didn't tell me where Kejun's first army posting was. Perhaps she didn't know. What she did say was that he was away for two years.

I asked her whether she and Kejun wrote to each other. Shu Wen gave me one of her hard looks that made me ashamed of my ignorance.

"What kind of postal system do you imagine there was?" she asked. "War had created enormous upheaval. All over China, women were longing for news of husbands, brothers, and sons. I was not the only one. I had to suffer in silence.

"I heard nothing from Kejun for two years. Separation was not romantic, as I had imagined—it was agony. The time crawled past. I thought I was going to go mad. But then Kejun returned, decorated with medals. His unit had sent him back to Nanjing to take an advanced course in Tibetan language and medicine.

"Over the next two years our love grew stronger. We talked about everything, encouraging and advising each other. Life in China seemed to be getting better day by day. Everybody had a job. They worked not for capitalist bosses but for the government and the motherland. There were free schools and hospitals. We were told that, through Chairman Mao's policies, China's economy would catch up with those of Britain and America in only twenty years. We also had the freedom to choose whom we would marry, rather than obeying the choices of our parents. I told Kejun about how our friend Mei had, to everyone's surprise, married Li, an unsophisticated country boy, and how Minhua, who seemed so meek, had eloped with Dalu, the head of the student council. Their parents had come to the university to complain. But I didn't tell him how, while he was away, I had had other admirers, and people had advised me not to pin my hopes on a man who risked death on the battlefield."

"WHEN KEJUN finished his studies, we decided to get married. He was awaiting orders from the military headquarters in Nanjing. I was working as a dermatologist at a big Nanjing hospital. In the eyes of our friends, many of whom had children, we had already waited late enough to marry. Kejun was twenty-nine, I was twenty-six. So we applied to the Party for permission. Although my father found it difficult to get used to the idea of free choice in marriage, he was very fond of Kejun and knew I had made a good decision. In any case, if I delayed marriage any longer, he would lose face. My older sister had already got married and had moved to Suzhou, taking my parents with her.

"Our wedding was celebrated in true 'revolutionary style.' A high-ranking political cadre was the witness and friends and colleagues wearing little red paper flowers were our escorts. For the refreshments we had three packets of Hengda cigarettes and some fruit candies. Afterward we moved into the hospital's married quarters. All we owned were two single wooden plank beds, two single quilts, a rosewood chest, a red paper cutout of two 'happiness' characters, and our marriage certificate decorated with a portrait of Chairman Mao. But we were ecstatically happy. Then, only three weeks later, Kejun's call-up papers arrived. His unit was to be posted to Tibet.

"We hardly had time to absorb the news before he left. The army arranged for me to be transferred to a hospital in Suzhou so that I could be close to my parents and sister. We hadn't requested a transfer but the Party organization said that it was only right that army dependents should have their families to look after them. I threw myself into my work so that I didn't think about how much I was missing Kejun. At night, when everyone else was asleep, I would take out Kejun's photograph and look at his smiling face. I thought all the time about what he had said just before he left: that he'd be back soon because he was anxious to be a good son to my parents and a good father to our children. I longed for him to return. But instead I received a summons to the Suzhou military headquarters to be told that he was dead."

We sat in silence together for some time. I did not want to interrupt her thoughts.

THAT NIGHT, Shu Wen and I shared a room in the small hotel next to the teahouse. During the two days we spent together, she opened up to me in a way that I had hardly dared hope.

But a few days later, when I called the hotel in Suzhou, she had already left. In a panic, I contacted the man who had called me about her.

"I don't know where she's gone," he said. "The other day she sent me a packet of green tea via the rice seller to say thank you for introducing her to Xinran. She said she hoped you would tell people her story. Since then I haven't met her again."

It was not until I went to Tibet again in 1995 to make a documentary that I began to understand what it might be like to live there. I and my four cameramen were rendered speechless by the emptiness of the landscape, the invisible wind that swept across the barren land, the high boundless sky, and the utter silence. My mind and soul felt clean and empty. I lost any sense of where I was or of the need to talk. The simple words that Shu Wen had used— "cold," "color," "season," "loss"—had a new resonance.

As I wrote Shu Wen's story, I tried to relive her journey from 1950s China to Tibet—to see what she saw, to feel what she felt, to think what she thought. I deeply regretted having allowed Wen to leave without telling me how I could find her again. Her disappearance continues to haunt me. I dearly wish that this book might bring her back to me and that she will come to know that people all over the world are reading her story.

## 2

*I Can't Leave Him in Tibet, Alone*

> Death Notice
> This is to certify that Comrade Wang
> Kejun died in an incident in the east of
> Tibet on 24 March 1958, aged 29.
> *Issued by the Suzhou Military Office,*
> *Jiangsu Province, 2 June 1958*

Wen stood stunned on the steps of the military headquarters, the summer rain of the Yangtze delta monsoon drenching her hair and face.

Kejun, dead? Her husband of less than a hundred days, dead? The sweetness of those first days after their marriage lingered in her heart. She could still feel their warmth. Of those hundred days, they had only spent three weeks together. It was impossible that he was dead.

He had been so strong, so talkative, so full of life when he set out for Tibet. An army doctor wouldn't have been directly involved in the fighting. What "incident" was this? How did he die? Why could nobody give her any information? They had not even added a few words to testify that he died a revolutionary martyr as they always did for soldiers who fell in battle. Why not?

In the flood of buoyant "Reports of Victory from the People's Liberation Army on Entering Tibet," there had been no mention of an incident in which Kejun could have died. Staff at the military office responsible for comforting the widows and orphans of fallen soldiers had told Wen privately that they hadn't received any of the standard battlefield bulletins from Tibet.

Wen stood in the Suzhou street, unheeding of the rain. The busy life of the town continued around her, but she noticed nothing. An hour passed, then another. She was soaked in sorrow and bewilderment.

The chiming bells of Cold Mountain Temple called her back from her grief. Returning to the hospital where she worked, truly alone for the first time, a thought flashed through her mind. What if Kejun had simply been separated from his unit, like all those soldiers who were mistakenly reported dead when they were actually on their way home? Perhaps he was in danger or had fallen ill. She couldn't leave him in Tibet, alone.

THE IDEA, conceived in that chill rain, that she should go and find Kejun proved to be so powerful that, despite all the attempts of her family, friends, and colleagues to talk her out of it, Wen was determined to join her husband's regiment and travel to Tibet. She rushed around every government office she could find, tearfully thrusting her marriage certificate, Kejun's parting note, even his few personal possessions—his towel, handkerchief, and tea mug—at everyone she saw. "My husband must be alive," she insisted. "He wouldn't abandon his new wife and the future mother of his children."

At first the military officials she talked to tried to dissuade her from joining the army, but when they heard she was a doctor, they stopped protesting. The army was desperately short of doctors and many of the soldiers in Tibet were suffering from altitude sickness. Her qualifications as a dermatologist made her even more useful: there were many severe cases of sunburn because of the high altitude. It was decided that Wen should set out for Tibet immediately. The urgent need for doctors and her own eagerness to start looking for Kejun as soon as possible made the long training undertaken by her husband an unnecessary luxury.

The day came when Wen was due to leave Suzhou. Her big sister and elderly parents took her to the long-distance-bus station by the river. No one said a word. No one knew what to say. Her sister pressed into Wen's hand a shoulder bag made of Suzhou silk, without telling her what was inside; her father quietly placed a book inside her newly issued army rucksack; her mother tucked a tear-soaked handkerchief into the appliqué fastening of Wen's blouse. With tears in her eyes, Wen handed her marriage certificate to her mother. Only a mother could be entrusted with something so important. She gave Kejun's tea mug and towel to her father, knowing how much he loved his son-in-law. She then gave her sister—who knew all Wen's secrets—a package containing Kejun's correspondence and documents, along with their love letters.

Dark, gloomy clouds merged with cooking smoke from the white-walled, gray-tiled local houses and gently enveloped Wen's family as they watched her climb onto the bus. Through the shuddering picture frame of the bus window, Wen saw her family grow smaller and smaller, and finally disappear from sight. She took her last look at Suzhou:

the houses with little bridges over flowing water; the temples on the hillsides overlooking the water; the lush greens of the Yangtze delta. There were red flags everywhere, fluttering in the breeze.

When Wen opened the silk shoulder bag her sister had given her, she found inside five tea-boiled eggs, still warm; two pieces of sesame cake; a bag of pumpkin seeds; a bag of dried sweet-sour turnip slivers; a flask of tea; and a little note, the characters blurred by tears:

> *My dear little sister,*
>
> *My heart is heavier than words can say.*
> *Our parents are no longer young and can't*
> *bear much more sorrow in their lives, so*
> *come back soon. Even if you no longer*
> *have Kejun, you still have us, and we can't*
> *live without you.*
> *Be safe, take care!*
> *I am waiting for you.*
>
> *Your sister*

The book her father had slipped into her bag turned out to be *The Collected Essays of Liang Shiqiu*. These essays, with their ability to turn the happenings of everyday life into gems of wisdom, were her father's favorite reading. He had written an inscription on the title page:

> *Little Wen,*
>
> *Just as books are read one word at a time, roads are taken one step at a time. By the time you've finished reading your book, you and Kejun will be taking the road home.*
>
> *Your mother and father await your return.*

Wen folded her sister's note into a paper crane and, along with a small photograph of Kejun, placed it inside the book as a mark, then wrapped the whole thing in her mother's handkerchief. She'd been told that private property was forbidden on military expeditions, and so these few precious things were all she had to keep her memories alive.

The bus set off northward, along the Grand Canal, which linked Hangzhou with Beijing, bumping and jolting passengers whose excitement at the prospect of the journey, a rare event in their lives, had soon been replaced by fatigue. Gazing at the still waters of the canal, Wen suddenly remembered something her father once told her: that the 2,400-

year-old canal linked the Yangtze, the Yellow River, and many of China's other rivers, and that all of China's major rivers flowed west to east and had their source in Tibet. This was her first connection to Kejun, this cold, deep canal, its waters originating in the land of glaciers and snowcapped mountains that had swallowed up her husband. She remembered the intense happiness of her first days of marriage. Early each morning, she had roused her husband gently from his dreams with a cup of green tea by his pillow. Each night, she had been soothed to sleep by his caresses. To be separated even for a moment was painful to them. At work, Wen always carried in the pocket of her hospital coat a message that Kejun had written for her that day:

> *It's raining today. Please take an umbrella and my love. Then I'll have no need to worry, no matter where you are, no rain will soak your body . . .*

> *Yesterday you coughed twice, so today you must drink two cups of water, and this evening I'll make you a medicinal broth to clear your lungs. Your health is the heart of our home . . .*

*Wen, don't worry, the home we talked about yesterday will come. I will be a good husband to you, and a good son to your parents . . .*

*Hey, little girl, eat a few more mouthfuls of food, you're getting thin! I can't bear to see you fade away!*

Tears poured down Wen's face. The middle-aged woman in the next seat took Wen's handkerchief from the front of her blouse and placed it in her hand.

STOPPING AND starting for six days and five nights, the bus made its way northwest through a constant flow of vehicles, animals, and humans, before finally reaching Zhengzhou—a city near the Yellow River and China's largest railway junction. Wen had been instructed to report to the army base there, then continue her journey by train to Chengdu, and finally enter Tibet by the great Sichuan–Tibet Highway. She had heard that Kejun's unit had also entered the Tibetan plateau by this complicated route.

On arriving at the bus station, Wen was met by a

soldier from the nearby army base. She was warmly welcomed and taken to her quarters. All the arrangements seemed thorough: although the beds in the dormitory were just wooden boards balanced on stools and slept six, the quilts and pillows looked spotless. Compared to the filthy street outside the window with its whirlwind of dust and piles of rubbish, it felt like paradise. The soldier sent to meet Wen told her they hardly ever saw any female soldiers—most women they accommodated at the base were family members looking for their men. His comment reminded Wen that she was now a member of the People's Liberation Army, and no longer an ordinary civilian.

Behind a curtain of woven straw, Wen had a refreshing cold wash. She then changed into the uniform that had been waiting for her. As she tidied her hair, using a tiny shard of broken mirror stuck into the curtain, Wen pondered how well organized the army seemed. If it had been able to defeat the leader of the Nationalists, Chiang Kai-shek, why couldn't it provide her with any information about Kejun?

The mirror was too small to show her what she looked like in her new uniform. She wondered if Kejun would recognize her. Then the accumulated exhaustion of six days of shaking and jolting on the long road overcame her and, even though it was only five o'clock in the evening, she threw herself on the bed and fell into a heavy sleep.

The one and only military reveille that Wen would hear in her entire life summoned her from a sleep so deep that it had left no room even for dreams. Beside her, five still-sleeping women lay sprawled over the bed. They weren't wearing uniforms. Maybe they were administrative workers or women come to search for their relatives, thought Wen. When she sat up, another body rolled into the space she had left. No one else had been disturbed by the bugle, even though it went on for so long. They must have been more exhausted than she was. Not even a bomb would wake them, she thought.

Feeling that she'd regained a lot of her strength, Wen got down from the communal plank bed to discover that the new uniform she was wearing had been crushed into a mass of creases and wrinkles. If Kejun could have seen her, he would have given her a tap on the nose—the punishment he had meted out whenever Wen hadn't been able to answer one of his questions. She had loved this "punishment" of hers. One touch of Kejun's hand would suffuse her entire body with warmth. Often, she used to fudge her answers on purpose.

"Sleep well?" A man greeted her with a smile from the doorway, interrupting her thoughts. Wen could sense immediately from his bearing, and from the firm and direct way in which he had addressed her, that he was an official.

"I—I slept very well. Thank you," she answered nervously.

The man introduced himself as Wang Liang and invited her to come and have breakfast.

"I can hear your stomach grumbling," he remarked. "The soldier who brought you here said you didn't come out of your room after your wash. Later on, a female comrade reported you were fast asleep, so we didn't wake you for dinner. In times of war, a good night's sleep is too precious to disturb."

Wen warmed immediately to Wang Liang.

She ate her first northern-style breakfast: a bowl of hulatang—a glutinous soup made from wheat flour mixed with coarsely chopped pickled greens, pig's offal, and lots of chili powder; there was also a cake of maize flour, very harsh to the mouth, and a lump of a very salty pickle made from mustard leaves, which they call "geda." These crude, spicy flavors would normally have been bitter medicine to a southern girl weaned on more refined substances, but Wen's stomach seemed already to have been disciplined by her military uniform and by hunger, and within minutes, she'd eaten her way through the helping of breakfast doled out to her, and knew she could easily polish off another two. But when Wang Liang asked if she wanted some more, Wen refused. Having read reports about the strict rationing still in force in the army, she knew that an extra helping for her would be snatched from the mouths of others.

After breakfast, Wen walked with Wang Liang to his office. Photographs of Mao Tse-tung and Zhu De in military uniform hung on the walls, giving the makeshift room an air of deep solemnity. The presence of a table and three chairs indicated that the office's owner had the authority to hold meetings. On the walls of the room were painted the Three Great Regulations and the Eight Principles of the Liberation Army in bright red characters. Wen was already familiar with these army slogans, among them "Obey all orders," "Do not take as much as a needle or a piece of thread from the masses," "Don't damage crops," and "Don't mistreat captives."

Seated at his desk under the portraits of the great leaders, Wang Liang seemed serious and imposing. With great firmness, he tried to persuade Wen to change her mind about going to search for Kejun. He urged her to put aside her feelings for her husband, and to consider the difficulties and the dangers she would face if she traveled to Tibet: she couldn't speak the language, she could easily lose her unit, the terrain and the altitude were making people ill, and the situation out there was extremely unpredictable. The casualty rates were high and, as a woman with no training, the chances of her surviving even a month were extremely low.

Wen looked Wang Liang in the eye. "When I married Kejun," she said, "I pledged my life to him."

Wang Liang bit his lower lip. He could see that Wen was not going to give up.

"You have a very stubborn heart," he said. "There is a military train going to Chengdu tomorrow. You may board it."

He handed her a booklet of military information on Tibet and Tibetan customs. Wen accepted them gratefully.

"Thank you, sir. I will study these hard during the journey and try to adapt to the conditions there."

"War gives you no time to study and no chance to adapt," Wang Liang remarked grimly as he got up and walked around to Wen. "It draws clear lines of love and hate between people. I've never understood how doctors manage to choose between professional duty and military orders. Whatever happens, remember one thing: just staying alive is a victory."

Wen sensed Wang Liang was trying to frighten

her. She nodded to show respect, but didn't understand what he had meant. She gave her sister's silk bag to Wang Liang: inside she had written the names of Kejun, her parents, her sister, and herself. She told Wang Liang that she hoped everyone inside the bag would be reunited in Suzhou. In return, Wang Liang gave Wen a pen and a diary. "Writing can be a source of strength," he said. Wen had spent less than an hour in Wang Liang's company, but his words were to remain with her throughout her life.

THE SO-CALLED army transport train turned out to be no more than a glorified goods train: each railroad car holding almost a hundred impossibly cramped people. The tiny windows, only twenty centimeters square, let in very little light. Wen, along with the only other female passenger, a nurse, was forced to huddle with the men. Before they got on the train, someone introduced the nurse to her: she was from Wenzhou and was eager to talk, but no one in the car, not even Wen, could understand what she was saying because of her thick Zhejiang accent. About once every four hours, the train would stop for five minutes in some desolate wilderness to give people a chance to empty their bladders and shake their arms and legs a bit. Sometimes, at night, it halted near a military supply station and they were given a proper meal, but otherwise, during the day the soldiers staved off their hunger pangs with biscuits and dry steamed buns.

To begin with, some of the soldiers were excited by the scenery whizzing past the tiny windows, but soon the lack of oxygen and the stifling heat inside the closed car sucked all the life out of them. Their only source of entertainment consisted in trying to get the Wenzhou nurse to produce her meaningless sounds. After a few hours of this, even she stopped talking.

Wen wasn't in the mood for conversation. Her thoughts were entirely caught up with her search for Kejun. She couldn't even face introducing herself to her fellow soldiers, terrified that the most basic question might send her into a state of emotional turmoil. She concentrated instead on reading the booklet Wang Liang had given her.

It spoke of nomadic tribes and the importance of religion in Tibetan culture. It was difficult to take in so much information and Wen's tired eyes kept closing.

FOR TWO days and two nights, the train rocked its silent passengers along their journey. It was early morning when it pulled into the large city of Chengdu. Wen was relieved to have arrived, for here she would find the recently built road that joined China to Tibet for the last leg of her journey. She was eager to see the road. She remembered the news reports when it had opened in 1954, proclaiming what an extraordinary feat of engineering it was. Joining Chengdu with Lhasa, a distance of nearly 2,500 kilometers, it was the longest road in China and the first proper road in Tibet. The four years it had taken to construct the road seemed short considering the number of mountains it had to cross, fourteen in all, and the rivers too, at least ten. The terrible snows and freezing winds that the laborers had had to bear were legendary.

ALTHOUGH AUTUMN was fast approaching, Chengdu was still enveloped in the humid, stifling heat of summer. Getting down from the train, Wen wiped her face with the sleeve of her sweat-soaked uniform. She could not imagine how shamefully dirty her face must be. It felt sore—rubbed raw by the continual wiping away of sweat during the journey. A huge number of soldiers were crowded on the platform, but the station was oddly hushed. The sardine-can conditions and lack of oxygen had exhausted everyone. Wen searched along the neat line of army placards on the platform, looking for the unit number she needed.

Eventually she found a notice bearing the number 560809 held up by a soldier with a startlingly youthful face. She fished out from an inner pocket her now rather damp military papers and passed them to the hand attached to the face. The face smiled briefly and the hand beckoned. Two weeks of travel with the army had taught Shu Wen the body language of soldiers like this one. As she staggered in the wake of the childlike young man she considered how, as a student, she had never thought to wonder how China's fifty-six groups and thousand regional accents managed to communicate when they got together. Now she realized the importance of gesture and the common language of human emotion.

Wen had imagined that once she reached Chengdu, she would be able to start making inquiries about Kejun right away, but when she joined Kejun's former unit she discovered that only the number 560809 remained the same: the whole unit had been re-formed, from officers down to foot soldiers, and no one knew exactly where the previous unit had been fighting in Tibet, let alone about Kejun's own particular section. A staff officer told her that, going by previous deployments, they might have been somewhere near the Bayan Har mountains in the unpopulated northeast region of Qinghai. However, information was scarce because there had been few survivors and those that there were had already been posted elsewhere. On the inside cover of her *Collected Essays of Liang Shiqiu*, Wen wrote down "Bayan Har mountains." Perhaps she would be able to find more detailed information about Kejun on the way to this place—although her heart went cold at the thought that there were few survivors. "My Kejun is alive," she recited to herself, over and over again.

There were two days of rest, reorganization, and instruction about going into Tibet. Wen and two other doctors were taught how to deal with some of the problems they would encounter, including altitude sickness. They were each given a portable oxygen tank and many spare cylinders. Goodness knows how I'm going to carry these around, thought Wen, if I begin to suffer from mountain sickness myself. Most of them had experienced a little altitude sickness already—a slight headache, a touch of breathlessness—but it was bound to get worse the farther they traveled into Tibet. The average altitude of "the roof of the world" was around 4,000 meters.

Finally Wen and her comrades-in-arms clambered into their army trucks and set off along the famous Sichuan–Tibet Highway. On their backs they carried their few possessions wrapped up in a quilt and bound onto a backpack with a cord. At night they would simply unroll their quilts and sleep on the ground.

The convoy was huge: several dozen trucks containing nearly a thousand men. Wen was overwhelmed by both the number of soldiers and the magnificence of the road. It was even more impressive than she had imagined. Endlessly twisting and turning, it took them through crowds of mountains. The weather was constantly evolving. One minute it was like a warm spring day with flowers in bloom, then suddenly white snow was flying around them. She felt as if she had entered a fairyland where a thousand years in the outside world passed in a single day.

Most of the soldiers on the trucks were young men of about twenty. They laughed noisily and punched each other as they discussed what little they knew of Tibet—the lamas, hermits, and nomads; the legendary cruelty of the people. Wen could tell that, beneath their bravado, they were nervous. They knew nothing of the conflict they were entering and rumors of the brutal physical

punishments that Tibetans meted out to their enemies abounded. Wen realized that most of these
young soldiers were uneducated peasants, utterly
incapable of understanding such a diverse, remote
people. She thought of Kejun's dedication to his Tibetan studies, his determination to master the
language. She squashed herself into a corner of the
truck and meditated on her goal: to find Kejun. Her
thoughts were like a cocoon and she barely noticed
the chatter of the other soldiers, the intense discom-
fort of the journey, the freezing cold nights, the extraordinary landscape. She was roused from her
reverie only when, after days of traveling along the
highway, the convoy of vehicles left the road and began driving over grassland that seemed to stretch
endlessly in all directions. Wen had no idea where
they were headed. She didn't even know if they were
driving north or south. She wondered if they would
be going anywhere near the Bayan Har mountains.
She hadn't been prepared for a landscape that
lacked any kind of landmark around which to orient oneself. They hadn't yet seen a single sign of human habitation.

The convoy was able to proceed only in stops and
starts, and cases of altitude sickness began to in-
crease. Some of the soldiers in the trucks cried out
that their heads hurt, some couldn't breathe prop-

erly, and some could hardly stand. As one of only three doctors in a convoy of more than a thousand soldiers, Wen had to rush back and forth with the portable oxygen tank on her back, teaching soldiers how to breathe, while feeding oxygen to those who were already semiconscious.

Just as people were beginning to acclimatize, Wen realized that something worse was happening. The convoy was slowing down and they could hear scattered gunfire in the distance. Sometimes they thought they saw human figures hiding behind rocks and thickets. They began to fear an ambush. Within a few days, the difficult terrain forced the convoy to split up and Wen's truck was left in a group of only seven vehicles. Although the area they were traveling through had allegedly already been "liberated" by the Liberation Army, there was hardly a local to be seen, no military units, and no signals accessible to the radio operators. Anxiety began to eat away at the soldiers on board the trucks as the emptiness of the mountains, the thinness of the air, and the violent changes in the weather enfolded them in a world of fear.

During the daytime they derived some comfort from the extraordinary scenery and the living creatures they spotted along the way—the birds and animals. But at night, with the dramatic drop in temperature, the sounds of animals, and the moaning of the gales through the trees, Wen and her companions felt caught halfway between this world and the next. Nobody knew what was going to happen. They expected death to strike at any time. They huddled together around their campfires and tried desperately to sleep. Wen lay awake listening to the wind. She seemed to hear Kejun's voice in the trees, warning her to be careful, not to get soaked by the dew or burned by the campfire, not to go off alone.

One morning, as the company woke at the light of dawn, the rigid corpses of two soldiers were discovered, gleaming Tibetan knives protruding from their breasts. The soldiers on sentry duty confirmed to each other in whispers that they hadn't heard a single thing all night long. The knives must have been thrown with incredible precision.

The next day, and the day after that, exactly the same thing happened: no matter how many watchmen they stationed, or how many fires they lit, the weary soldiers were greeted at dawn by two corpses stabbed with Tibetan knives. There could be no further doubt: they were being hunted.

Nobody could understand why only two soldiers were being killed each time. Whoever was doing this had chosen not to attack the whole convoy but to play a more dangerous game.

Because two of the dead were drivers and no one else knew how to drive, they were forced to abandon two of the trucks and crowd into the remaining vehicles. A deathly silence fell over the convoy. Wen knew that everyone was contemplating the sudden, violent fate that might become theirs.

Wen had no fear of death. She felt that she was drawing ever closer to Kejun. Sometimes she even hoped that she had entered the borderland between the living and the dead. If Kejun was already on the other side, she wanted to see him as soon as possible, no matter what manner of hellish underworld he was suffering in.

One afternoon, someone on one of the trucks pointed off into the distance, shouting, "Look— something moving!" True enough, in the direction he indicated, there was something rolling about on the ground. Wen saw one soldier about to shoot, but hurried to stop him. "If it was anything dangerous, it would have already attacked us, or run away," she reasoned. The company commander, who was on Wen's truck, overheard her. He ordered the truck to stop and dispatched a few soldiers to go and investigate. Soon they returned carrying the thing on their backs: it was an unimaginably filthy Tibetan, of indeterminate gender, covered all over with bright and jangling jewelry.

3

Wen gently cleaned away the grime to reveal a face with a warm, terra-cotta-colored complexion and sun-scorched rosy cheeks. It was a typical Tibetan woman's face, Wen realized—dark almond-shaped expressive eyes, a sensual mouth with a full lower and thin upper lip, and a straight, broad nose. But its youthful features seemed to have been ravaged by some terrible ordeal or illness—the eyes were bloodshot and listless, and from the sore and blistered mouth, the woman could only utter an exhausted slur of indecipherable sounds. She couldn't possibly have been involved in the recent night killings—a thought that had crossed Wen's mind—because she was barely alive.

A soldier passed Wen a flask of water, and she

poured its contents, drop by drop, into the woman's mouth. Her thirst quenched, the woman muttered two words in Chinese: thank you.

"She can speak Chinese!" a soldier yelled out to the assembled crowd of onlookers.

Everyone was very excited: this was the nearest to a Tibetan they'd ever been, and she spoke Chinese too. Immediately they all began to wonder whether she'd be able to help them prevent any more attacks, maybe by offering protection of some kind. Wen spotted the company commander glancing over in her direction as he conferred with officers from the other trucks. She supposed they must be discussing what to do with the Tibetan woman.

The commander walked over to Wen. "What's the matter with her? Will she be any use to us?"

Wen realized that the woman's life was in her hands. After taking the woman's pulse and using her stethoscope to listen carefully to her heart and chest, she turned back to the commander.

"I'd say she's just suffering from extreme exhaustion—she'll soon recover."

It happened to be the truth, but Wen knew she would have said the same thing even if it weren't. She didn't want to see the Tibetan woman abandoned.

"Get her onto the truck, then let's go." The commander climbed back on board without another word.

Once on the road, the Tibetan woman fell into a dazed sleep and Wen explained to her fellow soldiers that she probably hadn't eaten, drunk, or even slept for several days and nights. She could see that the soldiers didn't really believe her, but still everyone squeezed up to give the Tibetan woman as much space as possible.

Wen stared in fascination at the woman's necklaces and amulets rising and falling with her labored breathing. Her heavy gown, though coarse and covered with dust and dirt, was in places finely embroidered. This was no peasant woman, Wen thought. And then she smiled to herself as she suddenly realized that every soldier in the truck, some open-mouthed, couldn't take their eyes off this exotic creature.

WEN THOUGHT that day would never end. The road became increasingly rough and broken up as they slowly made their way through several precarious mountain passes. The wind gained so much strength that it rocked the trucks from side to side. At last they set up camp for the night in the shelter of a jutting rock. The commander suggested putting the woman close to one of the campfires—first, to give her the warmth she still needed but, more important, to deter the killers who had probably continued to follow them. They all settled down to a very uneasy sleep.

In the middle of the night, Wen heard the Tibetan woman give out a low moan. She sat up.

"What is it? Do you need something?"

"Water . . . water." The woman's voice sounded desperately weak.

Wen gave her some water as quickly as she could, then a generous portion of flour paste from the supplies. Earlier in the day, when they had first found the woman, Wen had only managed to give her a very small amount of food from her own rations, but now that they had set up camp and the provisions had been unpacked, she managed to put aside some more. Gradually the woman began to come back to life and was able to speak.

"Thank you," she said. "You are very kind." Although the woman spoke Chinese clearly, her accent was strange.

"I'm a doctor," said Wen, searching her mind for the Tibetan word for "doctor," which Kejun had once told her. "Menba. I can take care of you. Don't talk. Wait until you feel better. You're still very ill."

"There's nothing seriously wrong with me, I'm just exhausted. I can talk." With great effort, the woman shifted her limp body closer to Wen.

"No, stay there, I can hear you. What is your name?"

"Zhuoma," the woman said weakly.

"And where is your home?"

"Nowhere. My home is gone." The woman's eyes filled with tears.

Wen was utterly at a loss for words. After a brief silence, she asked, "Why can you speak such good Chinese?"

"I learned Chinese as a child. I have visited Beijing and Shanghai."

Wen was amazed. "I come from Suzhou," she said, excitedly, desperately hoping that the woman would know her hometown. But in an instant, Zhuoma's face was animated and full of anger.

"Then why have you left it to come and kill Tibetans?"

Wen was about to protest when suddenly the woman cried out in Tibetan. The men, who were already on edge, leaped to their feet. But it was too late: yet another soldier was dead, stabbed through the heart with a Tibetan knife. Shots and shouts rang out as a temporary madness descended over the soldiers. Then a terrifying quiet returned, as if a hideous fate were hanging over the first person to produce the tiniest sound.

Out of the silence, a soldier whipped around and pointed his gun at Zhuoma, who was still too weak to stand.

"I'll shoot you dead, Tibetan! Shoot—you—dead!" he screamed. He made as if to pull the trigger.

With a courage she didn't know she had, Wen threw herself between Zhuoma and the soldier.

"No, wait, she hasn't killed anyone, you can't murder her!" Her voice was trembling but firm.

"But it's her people who are killing us. I—I don't want to die!" The soldier looked as if he were about to explode with panic and fury.

"Kill her, kill her!" More and more soldiers joined in the argument. They were all on the side of the man with the gun.

Wen stared at the commander, hoping he'd come to her rescue, but his face remained stony.

"Good menba," Zhuoma said, "let them kill me. There's so much hatred between the Chinese and the Tibetans, no one can make things right again now. If killing me will bring them some sort of peace, I'm happy to die here."

Wen turned to face the crowd. "You hear that? This woman would sacrifice herself to you. Yes, she is Tibetan, but she likes us, she likes our culture, she's been to Beijing, to Shanghai. She can speak Chinese. She wants to help us. Why should we take her life just to make ourselves feel better? What would you think if people killed your loved ones for revenge? What would you do?" Wen was close to tears.

"The Tibetans have killed us for revenge," one soldier blustered.

"They have reasons for resentment and so do we, but why must we make things worse and create new hatreds?" As soon as the words were out of Wen's mouth, she thought how pointless it was talking to these uneducated soldiers who knew only love and hate. Wang Liang had been right: war drew clear lines of love and hate between people.

"What do women know about enemies? Or hate?" shouted a voice from the crowd. "Just shoot the Tibetan."

Wen spun around to face the voice. "Who says I don't know about enemies? Or hate? Do you know why I left Suzhou and traveled thousands of miles to this terrifying place? I came looking for my husband. We'd only been married three weeks when he went to war in Tibet and now he's disappeared. My life is nothing without him." Wen burst into tears.

The soldiers fell silent. Wen's weeping was accompanied only by the rustling and popping of burning wood. Dawn was beginning to break and a little extra light was illuminating the camp.

"I know what it is to hate. If my husband is really dead, dead at the age of twenty-nine, I'm here for revenge, to find his murderers. But don't you think the people here hate us too? Haven't you wondered why we haven't seen any people here? Don't you think that perhaps it has something to do with us?"

Wen looked around at her silenced audience, and continued more slowly and deliberately.

"All this death over the last few days is a warning to us. I've been thinking about it a lot: I'm just as afraid, as full of hate as you are. But why are we here? Have the Tibetans welcomed us? We've come to liberate them, but why do they hate us?"

"Company, fall in!"

The commander interrupted Wen. As the soldiers got into line, the commander whispered to her, "I understand what you're saying, but you can't talk to the soldiers like that. We are a revolutionary army, not a force for oppression. Get into line and await orders." The commander turned to the soldiers. "Comrades, we've found ourselves in a very complex and serious situation. We must remember the army's Three Great Regulations and Eight Principles, and the Party's policy on minorities. We forgive the misunderstandings of the Tibetan people, strive for their cooperation and understanding, and work as hard as we can for the liberation of Tibet."

The commander glanced over to Zhuoma and Wen.

"If we want to liberate Tibet, we need the help of the Tibetan people, especially Tibetans who can speak Chinese. They can lead us out of danger, win over the locals, and resolve misunderstandings. They can help us find water and places to camp, and teach us about the culture and customs of the Tibetans. The leadership has decided to take Zhuoma on as our guide and interpreter."

Everyone was stunned by this unexpected announcement, none more so than Zhuoma. Confusion was written all over her face. She plainly found it difficult to understand the commander's heavy Shanxi accent or what he meant by the army's regulations and principles, but she realized that the soldiers had stopped looking at her with such fierce hatred. With no further explanation, the commander dispatched soldiers to bury their dead comrade, light the stoves for breakfast, put out the campfire, and check over the weapons store. Yet again the murdered man had been a driver, and so another truck had to be abandoned. The remaining trucks were now more crowded than ever. Before the convoy set off, the commander arranged for Zhuoma and Wen to sit together in the cab of the truck, where he usually sat. He said it was to allow the soldiers "a bit more room," but Wen knew he wanted to give her and Zhuoma an opportunity to rest safely.

For the first part of the journey Zhuoma drifted into a long sleep, her head on Wen's shoulder. When she woke up, Wen was pleased to see that life had begun to return to her eyes. Wen made her eat a little more flour paste, and as Zhuoma's cheeks regained some color, she saw how young and beautiful she was.

"Where is your family?" asked Wen. "Where were you going?"

Zhuoma's eyes were filled with sadness. As the truck jolted along, she quietly told Wen the story of her life.

ZHUOMA WAS twenty-one. Her father had been the head of an important, landowning family in the Bam Co region, a fertile area just north of Lhasa that was one of the gateways through the mountains, providing access to the north of Tibet. He presided over a large household with extensive lands and many serfs. Zhuoma's mother had died giving birth to her, and her father's other two wives had not produced children, so she had been her father's greatest treasure.

When she was five years old, two Chinese men in military uniforms had come to stay in their household. Her father said that they had come to research Tibetan culture. It was only later that Zhuoma learned that they had been envoys sent by the Nationalist government in China to research the arts and customs of Tibet. The two Chinese had taken a great shine to her and, in their halting Tibetan, had told her many fascinating stories. The older of the two had preferred stories to do with Chinese history. He had told her about how five thousand years ago Da Yu had stopped the Yellow River from flooding by dividing it into two branches; how Wang Zhaojun, one of the Four Beauties of Chinese history, had brought peace to the north of China by marrying a barbarian king; how the principles of political power were contained in a book called *The Three Kingdoms*; and how Sun Yat-sen had founded the modern state of China. The younger man had entranced her with Chinese legends and stories of female daring. He talked of Nu Wa and how she had held a stone up to a hole in the sky when she saw it was broken, the Monkey King, who had challenged the authority of the heavens, and the young girl

Mulan who had disguised herself as a man and joined the army in the place of her father, remaining undetected for many years.

Zhuoma had been enthralled by these tales, which were utterly different from anything in Tibetan culture. She pestered the two men endlessly, until they began to tell everyone that Zhuoma asked more questions than there were stars in the sky. With their encouragement, she learned to read Chinese characters, although she hadn't wanted to write them herself, intimidated by the difficulty of copying the many pictures. The men had returned to China the year Zhuoma turned fifteen, taking with them many scrolls in Tibetan and leaving behind for her a huge pile of books, as well as a great loneliness and yearning for China.

As she was growing up, she would constantly beg her father to let her visit China, but he always said no, arguing that she was too young, or that it wasn't a convenient time. But when she heard her father telling people that he was planning to emulate other landowners and send her to study in England because of the historic links between the two countries, she threatened never to marry if he did not let her see Beijing. Her father relented and allowed her to accompany an estate owner from a neighboring region on a trip to China. Since she could speak

Chinese, this man had agreed to take her along, on the condition that she obey the sacred Tibetan law not to speak about what she knew and not to ask about what she didn't know.

And so the young Zhuoma went to Beijing in springtime.

"The people and the traffic terrified me," Zhuoma told Wen. "I'd thought of Beijing as another great grassland, like Tibet, with a different language and culture, of course, but no more than that. It was a huge shock. I couldn't believe how much the Chinese talked. Their faces seemed so white and clean, completely unmarked by life. There were no horses, no grass, no space, only buildings, cars, people, streets, and lots of noise. And Shanghai shocked me even more. I saw creatures with golden hair and blue eyes—like the ghosts you see in Tibetan paintings—just walking along the streets. Our Chinese companion explained that they were 'Westerners,' but I didn't know what he meant and couldn't ask because I had to keep my promise not to ask about 'what I didn't know.' "

When Zhuoma returned to Tibet, she was dying to tell people about all the strange and exciting things she had seen, but no one understood what she was talking about. Her father seemed to have something very serious on his mind. His permanent anxiety and gloom robbed him of all interest in what she had to tell him, while his two wives never talked to Zhuoma anyway. To compensate for his neglect, her father began to send his groom to keep her company and listen to her stories.

"My father couldn't bear to see me so lonely, but all he could think of doing to help was to send me one of his servants. It never entered his mind that I might fall in love with the groom."

A shadow of anguish passed across Zhuoma's face.

"My father was furious when he found out. He told me that what I was experiencing was not love but simply need. All I knew was what I felt: that I wanted to be with this man all the time, and that I loved everything about him.

"In my area of Tibet," Zhuoma continued, "love between a noble and a servant is forbidden. It is the will of the spirits, and there is nothing anyone can do to change that. But we are all creatures of emotion, and emotions are not so easily circumscribed. Because of this there are certain rules in place. If a male servant and a noblewoman fall in love, then the only option is for the man to take the woman far away. If he does this, she loses everything: family, property, even the right to exist in her native place.

My father knew I was stubborn so he took the advice of the family retainer, who had been his counselor since he was a child, and sent me back to Beijing with a group of servants."

The man who had first taken Zhuoma to China had Chinese friends in Beijing and the seventeen-year-old Zhuoma went to stay with them. Soon afterward her servants were ordered home. They could not cope with their alien surroundings. To them Beijing seemed not to belong to the human world at all. They felt surrounded by demons. No one spoke their language or ate their food. Without temples or monasteries they were completely unprotected by the spirits. Zhuoma, on the other hand, thrived. She enrolled at the Central Institute of Nationalities—a university set up by the Communist government specially to educate young people from China's minority territories. There the groom was soon replaced in her young mind by her love of Chinese culture.

"I loved meeting people so different from Tibetans," Zhuoma confided to Wen. "I loved Beijing, with its huge Tiananmen Square. At the institute, my Chinese was already much more fluent than that of most of the other minority students and I progressed well in my studies. At home I had never traveled beyond the confines of my father's land and

I was excited to learn that the various regions of Tibet had many different customs and many branches to its one religion. When I graduated, I decided to stay on as a teacher and translator of Tibetan.

"But it was not to be. Just as I was in the process of moving from the students' to the teachers' dormitory, I received a message that my father was seriously ill."

Zhuoma described how she had set out for Tibet that same evening, traveling as fast as she could day and night, first by train, then by horse and cart, and finally on horseback, whipping on the horse in her haste to return to her father's lands. But when she arrived at the foot of the Tanggula mountains, servants, who had been waiting for her there, broke the news that their lord hadn't been able to hold out for a last sight of his daughter. He had died seven days earlier.

Overwhelmed by grief and disbelief, Zhuoma made her way home. She could see in the distance the prayer flags fluttering from the hall where her father lay in state. When she came nearer she heard the chants of the lamas who would send her father's spirit to heaven. Inside the hall, her father was already wrapped in a shroud, with his two wives kneeling silently to his left. On his right was a portrait of Zhuoma's dead mother with the jade Buddha amulet she had used while alive. The gold-embroidered hassock Zhuoma used to pray on had been placed beneath the golden statue of the Buddha that sat at her father's head. He was surrounded by offerings to the spirits, white khata prayer scarves, sacred inscriptions, and other objects brought as tributes by friends, relatives, and the household and farm serfs.

"I was my father's heir," Zhuoma explained. "As a young woman, I had never thought about my father's duties as the head of such a large estate. Nor had he ever talked to me about such matters. But now, after the forty-nine days of burial rites had been observed, my father's retainer took me aside and explained to me the heavy burdens that had been my father's in the weeks before he died.

"He showed me three letters. One was from another local governor urging my father to support the Army of Defenders of the Faith and rise up against the Chinese. It said that the Chinese people were monsters and were bringing shame upon the lands of the Buddha. The letter told him to contribute silver, yaks, horses, cloth, and grain to the army and to poison the water sources to deprive the Chinese of sustenance.

"The second letter was from a Chinese general named Zhang who wanted my father to help 'unite the motherland.' He said that he hoped my father would help him to avoid bloodshed but that, if he did not, he would have no choice but to send soldiers onto his land. He told my father that I was being well cared for in Beijing.

"The third letter was from my father's fourth brother. It had arrived just before my father died. My father's brother advised him to flee west with his family, saying that in his region fierce fighting had broken out between Tibetans and Chinese. All the temples were destroyed, the landowners slaughtered, and the serfs fled. He had heard a rumor that I was being held captive in Beijing. He hoped his letter would arrive in time. He himself was awaiting his fate.

"On reading these letters I was thrown into confusion. I did not understand why there should be so much hatred between my homeland and my dreamland. I realized that my father's death must have been caused by his great anxiety. He was caught between threats from both the Chinese and the Tibetans. He would not have been able to bear the scenes described in my uncle's letter. Religion is the lifeblood of the Tibetan people.

"For hours I thought about what to do. I had no desire to help the Army of Defenders of the Faith kill Chinese people, nor did I want the blood of my own people to pollute the land. My property and my role as head of the estate meant little to me any longer. And so I decided to walk away from the fighting in the hope of finding freedom . . ."

Zhuoma went on to describe in a quiet voice how she had dismantled her estate. Having sent her stepmothers away with great piles of gold, she let the household servants go free and divided much of her property among them. The ornaments and jewels that had been in her family for generations she concealed in her clothing, hoping they would protect her and allow her to buy food in days to come. Then she opened the granaries and distributed their contents among the serfs. She sent the household's precious golden Buddha and the other religious objects to a monastery. All the time she was conscious of being watched by her father's retainer. He had been with the family since her father was three and had begun to learn the scriptures. Three generations of her family had benefited from his wisdom and resourcefulness. Now he was forced to witness the destruction of the household.

When all was done, Zhuoma walked through the house surveying its empty rooms. It was dusk and she carried a flaming torch. Before she left, she intended to burn the house down. As she was about to set the building alight, her retainer approached her, his head bent.

"Mistress," he said. "Since in your heart, this house is already burned to ashes, will you leave it to me?"

Zhuoma was taken aback. It had never occurred to her that this servant would ask such a thing.

"But there is nothing here," she stammered. "How will you live! The fighting is getting nearer . . ."

"I came here with empty hands and I will leave with empty hands," said the man. "The spirits will direct me. Here I was received into the Buddhist faith. In life or death my roots are here. Mistress, please grant my request."

All the time that he was speaking, he did not raise his head.

Zhuoma looked at him. She realized that this man was not the lowly servant of her childhood. His face was utterly changed.

"Very well," she said, feeling the gravity of her words. "May the spirits protect you and bring you your desire. Raise your head and receive your home."

With this, she passed him the torch.

Zhuoma led her horse to the gateway of the

courtyard, counting each step as she went—599 in all. When she reached the gate, she turned around and, for the first time in her life, realized how imposing her childhood home was. The two-story decorated archway was resplendent with bright colors; the workshops, kitchens, servants' quarters, stables, storehouses, and granaries to either side were beautifully maintained. Far off in the distance, her father's retainer stood like a statue, illuminated by the torchlight.

She turned out of the gatehouse and in what was left of the daylight noticed a man and a horse, the horse heavily laden with baggage.

"Who's that?" she asked in surprise.

"Mistress, it's me," came the reply. The voice was familiar.

"Groom? Is that you? What are you doing here?"

"I . . . I wanted to be a guide for my mistress."

"A guide? How do you know where I want to go?"

"I know. I knew it when my mistress came back from Beijing and told me stories."


ZHUOMA WAS so moved she didn't know what to say. She had never thought the groom was a man of such feeling and passion. She wanted to see his expression, but he spoke with a lowered head.

"Raise your head and let me look at you," she said.

"Mistress, your groom does not dare . . ."

"From now on, I am no longer your mistress and you are no longer my groom. What is your name?"

"I have no name. I am simply 'Groom,' like my father."

"Then I will give you a name. May I?"

"Thank you, Mistress."

"And you must call me Zhuoma, or else I will not have you as my guide."

"Yes . . . no," the man mumbled in confusion.

ZHUOMA SMILED as she told Wen how she had named the groom Tiananmen after the great square that had so impressed her in Beijing. But her expression soon turned to sadness as she described what had followed.

As she and Tiananmen were preparing to ride away from the house, Tiananmen suddenly pointed to the sky and cried out.

"Mistress, a fire! A great fire!"

Zhuoma turned to see her house ablaze and, in the courtyard, her family retainer howling prayers as he burned. The tears ran down her face. Her family's loyal servant was immolating himself in the house to which he had sacrificed his life.

Wen held her breath as she imagined what it must be like to lose one's family like that. As Zhuoma continued with her story, she was barely able to hold back the tears.

Zhuoma and Tiananmen had traveled east, toward China. Tiananmen was a good guide, taking them away from the usual routes and avoiding the conflict between the Chinese and the Tibetans. They had plenty of food—dried meat, barley, some butter and cheese. The rivers gave them water, and there was wood for the fire. Although they had to cross several high mountain passes, Tiananmen always knew where they could seek shelter. During the long journey, Tiananmen put his heart and soul into looking after Zhuoma: finding water, preparing food, collecting firewood, laying out the bedding, keeping watch at night. He overlooked nothing. Zhuoma had never before lived out in the open and didn't know how to help him. As she sat beside the leaping campfire or jolted along on her horse, she drank in his silent love. Despite their desperate situation, she felt hope and happiness. But then the weather changed. A great wind came over the steppe, bringing with it a blizzard that rolled up into itself anything it found before it. The horses were struggling badly, and Zhuoma and Tiananmen could only inch forward. Realizing it was too dangerous to continue, Tiananmen laid out a place for the exhausted Zhuoma to sleep in the lee of a huge boulder. He then positioned himself in the path of the gale to shelter her.

In the middle of the night, Zhuoma was awoken by the howling of the wind. She shouted for Tiananmen but there was no answer. She struggled to stand up but could not keep her footing in the gale, and instead crawled about searching and shouting. Lost in the pitch darkness, she lacked any landmark by which to orient herself. Finally she fainted and fell over a mountain edge into a rocky ravine.

When she came around from her stupor, the sky had been washed bright blue. Zhuoma was lying on the stony slopes of a gully. There was no sign of Tiananmen, his belongings, or any of their luggage. The blue heavens watched in silence as she wept; several vultures soared over her head, echoing her cries with their own.

"I shouted Tiananmen's name over and over again until my throat was hoarse," Zhuoma said. "I had no idea what to do next. Fortunately, I was unhurt, but I didn't know where I was or which way to go. I am the daughter of a nobleman: I am used to being looked after by servants. All I knew about east and west was the rising and setting of the sun. I walked for days without meeting a single person.

Then I collapsed with cold and hunger. Just as I thought I was going to die, I heard your trucks and I prayed to the Lord Buddha that you would see me."

THERE WAS a long silence in the cab of the truck. Wen didn't know how to speak to Zhuoma after all she had heard. In the end it was the driver of the truck who spoke first. Although he had appeared to be concentrating on the difficult road, he had heard every word.

"Do you think Tiananmen is still alive?" he asked.

"I don't know," replied Zhuoma. "But if he is, I will marry him."

THAT EVENING, everyone was afraid to sleep. Around the campfires, the exhausted soldiers sat back to back, with one group of men facing toward the fire, the other keeping watch over the darkness. Every hour they swapped places.

As they sat there, Wen remembered something. She turned to Zhuoma.

"When we were attacked this morning, you shouted something in Tibetan. What did it mean? How did you know the Tibetans had come?"

"I heard them whispering the ritual words that Tibetans utter as a signal to kill. I wanted to tell them not to do it, that there was a Tibetan in the group . . ."

Wen was about to ask more when Zhuoma cried out again, a piercing, desolate shriek that made everyone's hair stand on end.

As the cry died away, the people in the outer circle could see black shadows moving toward them.

Instinct told Wen that no one should move, that anyone who moved would be dead. Within a few seconds, countless Tibetans armed with guns and knives had surrounded them. Wen thought the end had come. Then a sorrowful song floated up into the air. The tune was Tibetan but the words were Chinese:

> *Snowy mountain, why do you not weep? Is*
> *your heart too cold?*
> *Snowy mountain, why do you weep? Is your*
> *heart too sore?*

Everyone watched Zhuoma as, continuing to sing, she slowly stood up and walked over to the leader of the Tibetans. Having first performed a Tibetan greeting, she drew an ornament from her gown and presented it to him. The sight of the ornament had an immediate effect on the Tibetan. He gestured to his men, who all took a step back. He then returned Zhuoma's greeting and started speaking to her in Tibetan.

Wen and the rest of the company had no idea what was being said, but they were sure Zhuoma was trying to work out a way to save them. After many tense minutes, Zhuoma returned. The Tibetans, she said, wished to punish them. On its way westward, the People's Liberation Army had extinguished the eternal flames in the monasteries and killed many of their herdsman. The Tibetans believed that 231 herdsman had been lost and they intended to take double that number of Chinese lives in compensation. Though Zhuoma had tried to negotiate with them, they refused to be merciful, arguing that to release the Chinese would allow them to kill more Tibetans. However, the Tibetan leader had said he would give them a chance if they agreed to three conditions. First, the Tibetans wanted to take ten Chinese as hostages, to be killed if the Liberation Army killed any more of their people; second, they wished the Chinese to return to their lands in the east and never to take another step westward again; third, the Chinese must leave behind all their weapons and equipment, including their trucks.

The radio operator argued that having to walk back with no food or water was no different from dying. Zhuoma told him that the Tibetans were prepared to leave them some dried meat.

All this time, the company commander had been very silent. Now he asked Zhuoma to return to the Tibetans and request permission for him to hold a meeting with his men. It was not long before Zhuoma came back. "They agree," she said. "You are to put your weapons on the ground and stand over there."

The commander unbuckled his gun belt, gently laid it on the ground, then turned to address his men.

"All Party members put their weapons on the ground as I have, and then follow me over there for a meeting. The rest remain here."

Twenty or thirty soldiers left the silent crowd, watched by the Tibetans. Several minutes later, some of the men returned to the ranks but twelve remained by the commander. The commander asked Zhuoma to tell the Tibetans that, although they had requested ten hostages, twelve Party members wished to live and die together. They would therefore provide an additional two hostages. Clearly moved by the self-sacrifice of the two extra hostages, the Tibetans gave the departing Chinese not only the promised meat, but a few waterskins and knives.

The two women remained behind with the Tibetans. Wen had told Zhuoma something of her search for Kejun and her desire to head north toward Qinghai. Through Zhuoma's influence, the leader of the Tibetans had agreed to let them accompany his men westward. When the time came for the women to go north, he would give them a guide. As Wen sat behind Zhuoma on one of the Tibetans' horses, clinging to her waist for dear life, she asked how Zhuoma had managed to negotiate with the Tibetans. Zhuoma explained that her ornaments identified her as the head of an estate. Although Tibetans were divided into many different groups, each with its own culture and customs, they all made sacrifices to Buddha, and all leaders had identical ornaments, which were a symbol of their power. The leader of the Tibetans had immediately recognized her superior status. She was glad to have been able to use her power to help Wen, because she owed the Chinese menba her life.

The group journeyed west for four and a half days. The leader then came to Zhuoma and Wen and told them that if they still wished to go to Qinghai, it was here that they should head north. They had just stopped to pack food and water for the women when three messengers on horseback came flying toward them reporting that the Chinese cavalry was up ahead. The Tibetan leader immediately ordered his men to hide their horses in the undergrowth nearby and Zhuoma guided their horse to follow.

In the thicket, Wen could not help being excited at having come across Chinese forces so unexpectedly. Perhaps Kejun would be among them. Her elation was soon quelled by the fury on the faces of the Tibetans, and the sight of the twelve Chinese hostages being led into a mountain pass. Terrified, she watched as a large unit of Chinese cavalry pursued and killed the few Tibetans who had not hidden themselves quickly enough. Gunfire was all around. Men fell from their horses, spouting blood. Wen grasped Zhuoma's hand, trembling at the gruesome scene. The Tibetan woman's hand was clenched.

Light drained from the sky. When the Tibetan leader finally gave the order that it was safe to move on, it was pitch-dark. Wen could feel the anxiety in Zhuoma's body as she urged their horse to keep up with the rest. But the wind and the darkness conspired to separate them from their companions. As they struggled onward through the gale, the horse suddenly gave a long, frightened whinny and threw them from its back. Seconds later they heard a thud as its body hit the bottom of a ravine. By throwing them, it had loyally saved them from certain death. Stunned, they sat with their arms around each other in the wild wind, hardly able to believe they were still alive. Wang Liang's words flashed through Wen's mind: "War gives you no time to study and no chance to adapt."

## 4

A TIBETAN FAMILY

Still floating somewhere between life and death, Wen struggled to open her eyes. She was lying on the ground, but she was warm and comfortable. A shaft of strong light was beating down from above, making it difficult to see anything around her. With great effort she moved her weak body. Instinct told her that every part of her was there, but her head felt strangely absent.

"Is this the sun of the human world," Wen asked herself, "or the holy radiance of heaven?"

A familiar face was bending over her.

"How are you, menba?" It was Zhuoma.

"Zhuoma?" Wen could feel herself returning to the land of the living. "Where are we?"

"We are in the home of a nomad family; this is their tent. Luckily for us, we had walked to the edge of the lowlands, where they have spent the winter. You collapsed. I don't know what I would have done if Gela, the head of the family, hadn't noticed us."

Wen tried to heave herself up.

"Don't move," Zhuoma warned. "They've put some ointment on your forehead. How are you feeling?"

"My pack . . ." Wen felt around the ground where she was lying for the bundle of possessions that she had carried so carefully from Zhengzhou.

"It's lost," said Zhuoma. "But the book you were carrying in your pocket is safe. I've put it beside your pillow. It must mean a lot to you. Even when you were unconscious, you were holding on to it."

A young girl of eleven or twelve entered the tent carrying an earthenware bowl, shyly handed it to Zhuoma, then ran back out again. Zhuoma told Wen that the bowl contained freshly drawn water, brought in by one of the daughters. The rest of the family were outside the tent working. They were planning to move on to spring pastures shortly, but in the meantime Wen could stay here and rest.

"But how can I possibly impose myself on these people?" Wen asked. "Surely they have enough difficulties in their life without the burden of a sick person."

"The Tibetan people open their homes to all

travelers," said Zhuoma quietly, "whether they are rich or poor. It is the tradition of our country." Then she went out to talk further with the family.

As soon as she was gone, Wen opened her book of Liang Shiqiu's essays and drew out Kejun's photograph. Amid all this strangeness, he was still smiling at her. She then took the opportunity to gaze at the extraordinary dwelling in which she found herself. The four-sided tent was made from large pieces of coarse material woven from animal hair and supported by sturdy wooden pillars. At its apex was a skylight, which could be opened and closed by means of a flap. This was the origin of the shaft of light that had blinded Wen when she woke. Now she watched the smoke from the cooking stove dancing in and out of the light. The simple stove, made from a large, boat-shaped stone raised from the ground on two small rocks, sat in the center of the tent. Beside it were a pair of bellows and stacks of brightly painted bowls, dishes, and jars, along with a few household items Wen could not put a name to. On one side of the tent, Wen spotted what must be the family's altar. Above a table set with religious objects hung an image of a Tibetan Buddha embroidered in colored brocade. To the right was a large cylindrical object made of bronze. Farther along there was a heap of felts and rugs, quilts and clothes. And on the other side of the altar, sacks filled with something that smelled like animal dung were piled high. The door to the tent was a flap through which an adult would have to stoop to enter. On either side of this flap were arranged a variety of household tools and equipment for animals.

From her bed on the ground, Wen tried to make some deductions about her hosts, but found it impossible to guess how well-off the family was from the many gold and silver hanging decorations, the battered tools, the large number of bowls and jars, and the limited bedding. Everything felt very new and strange to her, not least the peculiar odor of dung, sweat, and animal hide.

The sound of footsteps drifted in from outside and, for the first time in her life, Wen felt how peaceful it was to have one's ear to the grass and hear the sound of the human tread. When Zhuoma reentered the tent, she was surrounded by a crowd of people of all heights and ages. As Wen lay there looking up at their unfamiliar faces, her head swam.

Zhuoma introduced their hosts. There was Gela, the head of the family; his wife, Saierbao; and his brother, Ge'er. The family had six children but only four were present because two of the sons had entered a monastery. Wen found it impossible to follow the Tibetan names of the six children. They seemed even more inscrutable than the Latin names in the medical dictionary that she had never been able to memorize. Zhuoma explained that each of the names contained a syllable from the sacred mantra that every Tibetan uttered hundreds of times each day: Om mani padme hum. She suggested that Wen just call each child by the single syllable from the mantra: this would make the oldest son Om and the next son, who was at the monastery, Ma. The two daughters would be Ni and Pad. Me would refer to the other son who had gone to a monastery, and the youngest son would be Hum. Wen asked Zhuoma to thank the family for her and watched their shy smiles as Zhuoma translated.

Over the following weeks, Wen was nursed back to health by Gela and his gentle wife, Saierbao, who fed her milk tea mixed with herbal medicine every day. Zhuoma told Wen that the family had delayed moving to their spring pastures until she was fit enough to manage the journey.

The two women discussed at length how they should proceed in their search. Zhuoma thought that they should stay with the family until the warmer weather came. By summer, they would both have learned enough to survive outdoors, and the family would have built up their reserves of food and might be able to spare them some provisions and a couple of horses. Wen was alarmed by the idea of such a long wait. What might happen to Kejun in the meantime? But Zhuoma reassured her. The family was planning to travel northward to find spring pastures. Perhaps, she said, they would meet other nomads or travelers on the journey who would be able to give them news of Kejun and Tiananmen.

Wen had no choice but to accept her situation, although, lying weakly in her bed, unable to join Zhuoma as she helped the family with their tasks, cut off from conversation by her inability to speak the language, each day felt endless. As she convalesced, she watched the Tibetan family's routines. She was struck by the rigorous order of their days, which seemed to follow a pattern that had remained the same for generations. Each member of the family went about their business with very little verbal communication. Everyone seemed to know their place and their days were filled to overflowing with jobs to be done.

Gela and Ge'er, assisted by the oldest son, Om, were responsible for important matters outside the home, such as pasturing and butchering their herds of yaks and sheep, tanning hides, and mending their tools and tent. Zhuoma told her that it was they who would go off and leave the family periodically in order to trade for household items that were needed. Saierbao and her two daughters did the milking, churned the milk for butter, cooked the meals, collected the water, and made the dung cakes that would provide heat, cooking fuel, and light for the tent. They also spun and made rope.

Wen was full of admiration for the skills that made the family's self-sufficient life possible, but was daunted by how much she had to learn. Even eating their meals involved learning a whole new set of rules. Except for the cooking utensils, there were no forks, spoons, or chopsticks in the tent. The only eating tool the family used was a ten-centimeter-long knife that hung from their waists. The first time Wen tried to use one of these knives to cut a hunk of mutton, she nearly speared her hand. The children, who had crowded around her in amused curiosity as if they were watching an animal at play, gasped with horror.

The family ate the same three meals every day. In the morning they "licked jiaka." A dough made from roasted barley flour and curds was heated on the stove and placed on one side of a bowl. Milk tea was then poured into the other half of the bowl. While they drank their tea, the family would turn their bowls so that the tea absorbed the jiaka, grad-

71

ually washing it away. There was no need for cutlery. The first time Wen was given breakfast, she drank all the tea in the bowl in one go and then asked Zhuoma how to eat the jiaka. Once she was used to it, however, she enjoyed the sensation of partly drinking, partly eating her food, and found a way to avoid burning her mouth.

The midday meal was "mixed." This involved making tsampa out of ground roasted barley and curds. Holding the bowl in one hand, Wen used the other to roll the ingredients into little balls. "Rub first, turn second, and grasp third," she would repeat to herself. The meal was always very generous: in addition to tsampa and milk tea, there would be dried meat boiled on the bone, which the family picked off with their knives. The little boy Hum showed Wen how to rip it apart with her hands and gnaw on it. There would also be delicious fritters fried in butter. Wen could see that this was an important meal for everyone: it could last for nearly two hours and the normally quiet family would spend some time discussing problems that had come up in the day. In the evening, the family ate meat and barley flour again, but cooked into a sort of gruel in a way that reminded Wen of the hula soup she had drunk in Zhengzhou.

Each meal was so health-giving and nutritious

that Wen's cracked skin healed and her cheeks became rosier every day. Already she could feel her body getting stronger and her skin becoming tougher as it adapted to the harsh winds, the cold, and the sharp sunlight. The family appeared to accept her presence, but they never tried to speak to her. They would talk only to Zhuoma, of whom they appeared to be in great awe. Later, Zhuoma would tell Wen what had been discussed. Excluded from all conversation, Wen sometimes felt like one of the family's animals: protected, gently treated, watered, and fed, but set apart from the human world.

The religious practices of the family made her feel even more of an outsider. They prayed constantly, muttering the mantra "Om mani padme hum" under their breath even as they worked. They frequently came together for prayer ceremonies where the father, Gela, would turn the heavy bronze cylinder above the altar by means of a length of rope and lead the family's incantations as they spun little wheels on sticks. Zhuoma explained to Wen that both the large cylinder and the smaller wheels were prayer wheels. She depended heavily on Zhuoma for explanations about everything and gave thanks that she had been fortunate enough to encounter such a brave, clever woman. Had it not been for Zhuoma, she could never have begun to understand this family who, with their deep spirituality and carefree self-sufficiency, was as different from the Chinese as heaven and earth.

Misunderstandings, though, were still frequent. In the rare moments that Wen found herself alone, she would take out Kejun's photograph and caress his smiling face. One day, the little boy Hum came into the tent when she had the photograph in her hand. He took one look at the picture and ran from the tent calling out in terror. Distraught, Wen went to find Zhuoma to ask how she had frightened the boy. Zhuoma explained that he didn't know what a photograph was and was afraid of the man "sleeping" inside it.

Eventually, the family felt that Wen had recovered sufficiently for them to move on. On the day of departure, Wen woke at dawn to see the shadows of Gela and Saierbao swaying in the weak light. She noticed that many of the things from the tent had been parceled up into rolls to be carried by the yaks. Because she hadn't yet learned to ride, Gela's brother, Ge'er, had made a kind of saddle shaped like a round-backed chair for her out of a few luggage rolls, so that she would not fall off her horse if she went to sleep. He indicated to her that he would take charge of her reins.

The path their journey followed was very hard going. Storms forced them to stop and they had to huddle among the yak herd. At night they slept in the open air, sheltered from the snow and wind by mountain rocks. They did not see another soul. Wen couldn't imagine who the "bandits" were that the Liberation Army had been hunting in this deserted area.

As the altitude, the hard riding, and the unfamiliar food began to gnaw away at her strength and spirit, she was plunged into depression. Was Kejun suffering as she did? And how would she ever find him in these snowy ice fields where she had neither language, survival skills, nor any means of transport? She had lost all sense of time. Each day was like the other and she did not know if they had been traveling for days or weeks. When finally they arrived at their destination, Zhuoma told her that they were close to the Bayan Har mountains and would set up their spring camp in the lush grassland near the Yalong River. For half a day, Gela and his sons hammered in poles, hung the tent, and secured the guy ropes. Once the tent was up, Saierbao and her daughters deftly arranged their household items. Wen sat by the luggage, clumsily helping them out with a few light tasks. Just as she was about to hand a prayer wheel to Saierbao, Zhuoma stopped her, warning her that outsiders shouldn't touch objects of worship.

According to their custom, after setting up house the family feasted on meat, tsampa, fritters, and barley wine. Just as she did while they were on the road, Saierbao prepared Wen some medicinal milk tea. After the feast, Gela led a prayer ceremony. That night, when they were all lying together on the ground, Wen wedged between Zhuoma and the daughter Ni, Zhuoma whispered to her that, as well as praying for the yaks and sheep to get fat and strong, Gela had prayed for the spirits to protect Wen. Wen was deeply moved and, when she thought no one was listening, quietly recited to herself the Buddhist mantra: Om mani padme hum.

The next day, helped by Saierbao, Wen put on a Tibetan gown for the first time. They were the "maiden's clothes" that Saierbao had worn before her marriage and consisted of a set of white undergarments made of a coarse cloth, a long-sleeved collarless shirt fastened at the side, and a pair of trousers, richly decorated and gathered in at the ankles. Over this, Wen put on a thickly lined robe of blue, pink, and purple cloth that hung all the way down to her feet. Saierbao showed her how to wrap it across the front of her body and secure it with a broad brocade belt. She then tied a rainbow-striped length of cloth rather like an apron to the front. Wen was still frail, so to help her withstand the cold mountain winds, Saierbao gave her a high-necked sheepskin waistcoat and some felt boots. The boots were far too big, but Zhuoma said that it didn't matter: in cold weather they could stuff a thick layer of yak's wool inside for warmth.

Finally, Saierbao tied a jade amulet to Wen's waist and placed a rosary of wooden prayer beads around her neck "They will protect you," explained Zhuoma. "They will keep evil at bay and drive away ghosts." Then she smiled and silently placed a string of her own carnelian beads around Wen's neck.

Saierbao made a sign to Wen to sit down, and standing in front of her, she parted her hair with a comb and made two braids on either side. The youngest daughter, Pad, who was standing to one side, then gestured to Wen to look at herself in a bowl of water she had standing ready. Wen could hardly believe her eyes: apart from the fact that her braids were too short because she had only shoulder-length hair, she looked like a proper Tibetan woman. She tucked her precious book containing Kejun's photograph and her sister's paper crane inside the big pocket of her Tibetan robe.

A few days later, Wen noticed that someone had

laid a cloth bundle on her sleeping space. It was her uniform, now cleaned and mended. Wen was so touched that she didn't know what to say. She held the clothes in both hands, inhaling the tang that came from the sun of the high plateau, and bowed deeply to Saierbao.

ZHUOMA TOLD Wen that Tibetans said there were only two seasons, summer and winter, because, in Tibet, spring and autumn were so brief. But that spring was a very long one in Wen's life: she spent many sleepless nights, longing for Kejun and turning over and over in her mind her uncertain future. She couldn't imagine how she could possibly continue to survive in such harsh conditions, or learn a language that seemed to her utterly impenetrable. Although she knew there must be other nomadic families in the region because Zhuoma had told her that Gela and Ge'er met other herders when they were out at the pastures, the women saw nobody. She began to doubt whether Zhuoma had been right in thinking there would be an opportunity to get information about Kejun and Tiananmen. Both she and Zhuoma were so absorbed in their struggle to adapt to the nomadic way of life that each had entered her own private world, and they rarely discussed what they would do next. Despite her loneliness, though, Wen had begun to feel great affection for the family, particularly its matriarch, Saierbao.

Saierbao's face was so weathered that it was hard to tell how old she was, but Wen guessed she must be about thirty. She was an extremely calm and dignified woman who seemed to savor all her chores, however tough and exhausting they were. She never shouted or scolded. Even if someone knocked over her freshly made tsampa or spilled her milk tea, she didn't get cross. At most she would purse her lips and smile briefly as if she had seen it coming. Saierbao loved jewelry and draped herself in precious things even on ordinary days: with her necklaces, bracelets, and waist ornaments of agate, jade, gold, and silver, she was like a multicolored wind chime. Wen rarely saw Saierbao rest: her tinkling began the moment the first rays of light sneaked into the tent; at night, the whole family took its cue for sleep when her chimes fell silent. Wen would imagine performing the routines of life with Kejun in the manner of Saierbao: bearing and raising children, husband and wife working together in harmony. But every night, as soon as the final movement of Saierbao's daily concert drew to a close, Wen was brought back with a jolt to her longing and isolation, and her face would be bathed in tears.

Gela seemed older than Saierbao. He was a man of few words, but was the spokesman for the family. One of the popular Chinese myths about Tibetans was that the men were tall and strapping, but Gela was not much taller than his wife. Neither fat nor thin, his face neither humble nor arrogant, happy nor angry, he gave an impression of reliability, but he was not an easy man to read. Even the animals, Wen discovered, recognized Gela's dignity and authority: no sheep would wander off, no horse would refuse to allow its hoof to be picked up when Gela was around. Everyone, human and animal, took their orders from Gela's body language: he was a model patriarch.

Ge'er was close in age to his older brother, Gela. The two were very alike, except that Ge'er was thinner. Wen found herself wondering whether he was a mute. He never spoke, not even when he was playing with Hum, the youngest child, of whom he was very fond. Zhuoma told Wen she'd heard Saierbao say Ge'er was the best craftsman in the family, and Wen often saw him mending tools with extraordinary concentration.

One night, just as daylight was breaking, Wen decided to brace herself against the gale and go outside the tent to relieve herself. When she tiptoed back past the sleeping family, she was amazed to see Saierbao under the quilt with Ge'er, their arms wrapped around each other. She stood there for some time, unable to move, watching them sleep.

Since coming to live with Gela's family, Wen had slowly gotten used to sharing a common bed with all of them, male and female. She couldn't imagine how husbands and wives conducted their sex lives in full view of all, but she knew a great many races had lived like this for centuries. It had never occurred to her that the calm, dignified Saierbao would have an affair with another man right under her own husband's nose. Just to live with your own husband, she wanted to shout to Saierbao, is the most precious, wonderful thing in the world. She didn't, of course, but nor was she able to go back to sleep.

The next day, Wen remained troubled by her discovery. She didn't know how to look Saierbao and Ge'er in the face and tried to avoid them. Everyone noticed there was something wrong with Wen, but assumed that she was homesick. Ni kept dragging Zhuoma over to try to persuade Wen to tell her what was wrong, but Wen just went red and they couldn't get any sense out of her. Zhuoma knew that Wen often stared into space during the day and wept at night, so she assumed Wen's distractedness must be due to missing Kejun and was afraid to risk asking clumsy questions.

After a few days, Wen's sense of embarrassment had faded a little. When she observed Saierbao and Ge'er together, she could see that the two of them acted as if nothing was going on. She very much wanted to find out whether they were really in love or whether their coupling was just a physical urge, but she was ashamed of her own nosiness. Still, however she looked at it, Saierbao no longer seemed such a paragon. For Gela—a man whose wife was being stolen from under his nose—she felt pity; for Ge'er—a man who was living under his brother's roof but flouted the most basic moral rules— disgust.

One day, the family's fifth child, Me, approached the camp on horseback in the company of a group of lamas from his monastery. He was on a trip to collect colored stone from the mountains, which could be ground into pigment for religious paintings. He had heard from neighboring nomads that the family was nearby. When he saw Saierbao and Ge'er he galloped toward them shouting, "Mother, Father." Since Gela was working away from the tent that day, Wen thought she must have misheard the form of address Me used. Her Tibetan was still limited to a few basic words. But Zhuoma, who had taken over churning the butter from Saierbao, said with a sigh, "Me must miss his mother and father. All children who leave home for the monastery get homesick."

"Yes. Such a pity his father's not here," Wen added sympathetically.

"Oh," said Zhuoma smiling, "that doesn't matter. For Tibetan children any of their fathers will do."

"What do you mean?" asked Wen, surprised. "Zhuoma, do you mean to say Gela and Ge'er are . . ." Wen stopped Zhuoma from turning the wooden pole.

Zhuoma was astonished by Wen's confusion until suddenly it dawned on her. "Didn't you know that Gela and Ge'er are both married to Saierbao?"

Now Wen was even more bewildered. "Saierbao has two husbands?"

"Yes, this is Tibet. In Tibet a wife can have several husbands. You never asked me about it so I thought you'd worked it all out from hearing the children call to them."

Zhuoma passed the butter pole to Ni, who was standing nearby, entranced by their talking to each other in Chinese, and pulled Wen to one side.

"I understand how difficult it is. For you, living here is just like being in Beijing was for me. If I hadn't visited China, I would still think the whole world lived on a snowy, mountainous plateau."

Now that she understood Saierbao's "adultery," Wen was ashamed of her own ignorance and misjudgment. She didn't tell Zhuoma that what she had seen a few nights ago had been the cause of her low spirits.

Wen was disappointed to find that Me and his fellow lamas knew nothing of the conflict between the Chinese and Tibetans and had not seen a single Chinese soldier. Just before they departed, Wen asked Zhuoma if Me might be persuaded to part with two small pieces of colored stone. That evening, she used one of the stones to write a letter to Kejun on the back of his photograph.

> *Dearest Jun,*
>
> *Are you all right? I just want to write one word. Sorry. Sorry to you because I haven't found you yet. Sorry to myself, because I can't search the plateau on my own. Sorry to Zhuoma and this Tibetan family, because I have no way of repaying them.*

The color from the stone pencil was very faint but the stone made such a deep indentation that her words were engraved on Kejun's smiling face. She remembered the diary and pen that Wang Liang had given her in Zhengzhou and that were now buried, along with her pack, somewhere in a mountain pass. "Writing can be a source of strength," Wang Liang had said. She felt that her short message to Kejun had given her fresh courage to face the difficulties ahead.

Me's brief visit to the tent made Wen reflect on what life was like for Tibetan children. It must have been very hard for him to leave the family at such a young age, she thought, and Saierbao must feel his absence deeply.

Zhuoma told her not to worry.

"The Tibetans let children go very easily," she said. "All of Tibet is like one enormous monastery. Every household with more than two sons has to send at least one to the monastery to become a lama. This shows their religious devotion, but it also gives the child an education and relieves the economic burden on the family. There is a Tibetan saying: 'Yak butter is a more lasting possession than a son.' This is because a yak belongs to a family alone, but a son can easily be taken away to a monastery."

Were Tibetan children allowed any kind of childhood at all, Wen wondered. She noticed that, except for clothes and hats, hardly a single item in Gela's household was made especially for children. She asked Zhuoma to question Ni about what it had been like when she was smaller. Had she ever had toys?

"Yes," Ni replied. Her father, Gela, had made her lots of toys out of grass and dried goats' tails, but whenever they moved on they had to be left behind. He had also carved them wooden animals as birthday presents.

The oldest son, Om, was no longer a child. He must have been about eighteen and spent the day silently working away with Gela and Ge'er. He couldn't read but he played the Tibetan lute beautifully and sang well. Every day at dusk, the time when all the family dealt with little bits of personal business, like removing lice from their robes and hair, washing themselves, or laying out their bedding, Wen would hear him singing outside the tent. She never knew what he was singing about, since it was all but impossible for her to communicate with Om, but she could sense a man's outpouring of feeling for a woman. Om's singing always brought out her longing for Kejun, as if the sound waves could shake him out of hiding. Wen had no idea how an eighteen-year-old boy raised in such isolation could create such resonant melodies.

The oldest daughter, Ni, had just reached puberty and was the most animated member of the family. She was like a merry little bell, able to make her usually taciturn parents rock with laughter. But Ni always cried secretly at night. At first, Wen thought Ni was having nightmares. When she tried nudging her awake, however, she found that Ni wasn't asleep. Wen didn't understand how the girl sleeping next to her could be so different by day and at night. She could see a kind of despair in Ni's tearful eyes. Wen avoided thinking about this. She herself was trying to hold off despair and refused to succumb to it even when, in her worst nightmares, she saw a blood-soaked Kejun. Wen wondered what had left this lovely, flowerlike girl so bereft of hope.

Ni's younger sister, Pad, was so quiet she hardly seemed to exist. Nevertheless, she was always close by to lend a helping hand, passing her mother or sister the very thing they were looking for. If, after the evening meal, Pad was seen pressing their belongings to the edge of the tent to keep out the draft, Saierbao would give everyone an extra blanket for the night and, sure enough, later Wen would hear the wind roaring outside the tent. Astonished by Pad's predictive abilities, sometimes Wen was tempted to ask Zhuoma if Pad might have some knowledge of Kejun's whereabouts. But she was too afraid of what she might learn from such a revelation. She didn't dare risk a forecast that could crush her hopes.

The little boy Hum seemed to be about eight or nine. He loved being around other people, always wanting to learn everything. Wen often watched him with Om, who was teaching him to play the lute. Om would show his little brother the fingering and how to pluck the strings by tying the little boy's fingers to his own as he played. Hum also liked to pull the butter-churning pole from his mother's hands, leaving Saierbao no choice but to place a pile of dung sacks under his feet so he could see how to stir the pole through the milk. He would even run into a flock of sheep his father was trying to round up, copying how his father threw the lasso and yelled at the animals. Zhuoma told her that Hum was eager to enter a monastery like his two brothers. Wen couldn't understand how a little boy who had never left home could be so keen to become a lama. She noticed that Hum prayed with a devoutness far beyond his years. Such maturity of belief in a boy not yet four feet tall must, Wen realized, be a true spiritual vocation.

. . .

EVERY DAY Wen noticed surprising things about the Tibetan way of life, and was constantly amazed by the differences between Tibetan and Chinese customs. One day, she discovered that Gela and Ge'er, not Saierbao, did all the family's needlework. The first time she saw Ge'er sewing a robe, she could hardly believe it.

"Zhuoma," she shouted, "come over here! What's Ge'er doing?"

Saierbao, who was standing nearby, couldn't understand Wen's reaction. What was so surprising about the men in the family doing the sewing? Zhuoma told her that Chinese men hardly ever touched a needle, that sewing and mending were invariably women's work. Ni fell about laughing after she heard this. "Women, sewing?" she said to her mother. "Surely not."

Saierbao shook her head, sharing in her daughter's disbelief at this absurd idea.

So, it was the men's stubby fingers that were responsible for the whole family's clothes and bedding, and even Om could sew a decent seam. Ge'er was particularly skilled with a needle and Wen learned that almost every item of ceremonial clothing the family possessed had been made by him.

Zhuoma explained that the clothes of the earliest people in Tibet had been made out of animal skins and furs, which needed to be sewn with very thick thread. Only the men had the strength to sew with needles like iron poles and ropelike thread. Although it was now possible for women to sew clothing, the old tradition remained.

WEN WAS eager to be able to repay the family's hospitality by helping them with their work. However, she rapidly discovered that, although Saierbao swayed and hummed as she went about her tasks, they were by no means easy.

At first she found it impossible to milk the yaks. It was a job that demanded a great deal of skill. Worn out and dripping with sweat, Wen got nothing but complaints, and certainly no milk from the yaks. Even Pad, who quietly passed her a cloth to wipe away the sweat, couldn't stop a little smile from crossing her face.

Making dung cakes looked easier but Wen soon found out that this was very deceptive. Before the dung could be dried, it had to be collected. She was supposed to scoop up the dung with a special curved shovel, and swing the droppings into a basket carried on her back. Then it had to be kneaded and patted into cakes, dried in the sun, neatly piled into sacks, and stored inside the tent. Wen usually ended up throwing the fresh dung all over herself instead of into the basket on her back. She howled at Zhuoma about how bad her aim was.

Being pure physical labor, fetching water required the least skill of all the chores. But it demanded great strength. Wen could hardly bear the weight of the water cask and would stagger along. More often than not, she would lose most of her load before she was halfway home.

Wen most wanted to master the butter churning. Saierbao said that her mother used to tell her that this was a woman's most exhausting task—but also one of the skills for which she was most respected, because butter (and the yogurt and curds that were made from what was left over) was the essential ingredient of all three daily meals. Churning involved stirring milk in a wooden tub with a wooden pole hundreds of times, until the fat separated and could be ladled off to make the butter. Another process involved separating the curds and whey. The dried curds could be made into cakes with tsampa and were often used as religious offerings.

The equipment and methods used in churning reminded Wen of the chemistry experiments she used to do at the university. However, after half a morning helping Saierbao, she could hardly raise her arms, and by evening, her hands were too weak even to pick up her food and eat.

Wen recalled her mother telling her that an educated young Chinese woman should have a thorough grounding in six things: music, chess, calligraphy, painting, needlework, and cookery. A Tibetan woman was valued for a very different set of accomplishments. Wen blushed at the thought of her own incompetence. Even her medical training was of little use here. The family made their own herbal remedies, very different from those in Chinese medicine. Zhuoma showed her the mysterious caterpillar fungus and the saffron crocus, which were of great medicinal value. She understood now why Kejun had needed to undergo special training in how to use Tibetan herbs.

Zhuoma was also suffering with the work. Although she had a better understanding of what was expected, she was not used to physical labor and tired easily. Gela was kind to the two women and told them not to expect too much of themselves. The four seasons allowed people to move their homes, and yaks and sheep to mate and molt. They should take life a day at a time.

. . .

ONE DAY, Ni bounded up to tell her mother that Om said the grasses were budding. Saierbao screwed up her eyes and sniffed, as if to seize hold of the smell of summer. She told Zhuoma that Gela would shortly give the order to move to summer pastures on higher slopes. Again they would be traveling northward. Wen was in awe of the family's understanding of the landscape. The concept of a map was utterly alien to them. They moved around by instinct, obeying the wisdom of ancient times: "In spring go to pasture by water, in summer on the mountains; in autumn go to pasture on the high slopes, in winter on the sheltered plains." She realized that even if a map of this uncharted terrain had existed, she wouldn't have been able to use it. She had absolutely no idea where she was and all the mountains and plains looked the same to her.

Everyone was excited at the thought of the summer move. The days had been growing warmer and longer, the sun was getting hotter and, at the midday meal, they would leave their fur jackets open. Wen, who was now comfortable on horseback, felt a new sense of self-confidence. She was sure that she was on the road to finding Kejun and imagined him bundled up in Tibetan clothing like her, struggling to survive and find his way home. She fantasized about a horseback reunion amid a flock of sheep and the pleasure of drinking milk tea with Kejun in a tent. She surprised Zhuoma with her happiness.


THEIR LONG trek north took them over the Bayan Har mountains to the northern foothills, where they set up camp on the lush, grassy slopes. To the north, Wen could see the snowy peak of an immensely high mountain. Through Zhuoma, Gela explained that it was Anyemaqen, a sacred mountain and the most important of the thirteen holy mountains at the source of the Yellow River. Anyemaqen was the god who watched over this region with its many lakes threaded onto the newborn Yellow River like pearls on a string. In ancient times the Tupo tribe called this area the Hundred Lakes, and nomads often still used this name.

"This is the place where Wencheng, the Chinese princess of the seventh-century Tang dynasty, married the Tibetan king Songtsen Gampo," Zhuoma added. "All Tibetans know the story of the alliance between China and Tibet. Wencheng introduced crops and medicines to Tibet, and showed us how to grow barley. The king and his bride honeymooned at the source of the Yellow River before making the arduous journey southward to the capital, Lhasa.

There Songtsen built the Potala Palace for his queen. In Qinghai there is a temple built to commemorate the arrival in Tibet of Princess Wencheng."

If I find Kejun, we'll visit that temple together, Wen told herself.

In all the time Wen and Zhuoma had been with the family, the men had never traveled away from the tent for more than a day, so Wen was surprised when she saw Gela and Ge'er preparing to set off on a long journey. They were taking with them yaks and sheep, along with two white khata scarves from the store that the family kept as offerings. She asked Zhuoma where they were going.

"They are going to visit a stonecutter who will engrave the mani mantra into stone for them so that they are protected from evil and will prosper," Zhuoma replied. "Have you noticed that we often pass boulders engraved with words and pictures?"

Wen had indeed been puzzled by the inscriptions she had seen on rocks, and the piles of smaller, carved stones that she saw everywhere. However, she had taken to heart the Tibetan taboo not to ask questions about religion and had not dared to raise the subject. The more time she spent with Gela's family, the more moved she was by their spirituality, so she was pleased when Zhuoma offered to tell her more about the mani stones while they walked to collect water.

Since their first long conversation in the cab of the army truck, Zhuoma and Wen had avoided talking too much about politics and religion, as if frightened that their growing friendship might be spoiled. But now, Zhuoma seemed eager to explain Tibet's religion to Wen, as if in recent days she had developed a new trust in her.

"There are some men," she said, "who feel a strong spiritual calling to go and live on sacred mountains and spend every day selecting rocks or rock faces in which to carve the mani mantra. Usually, whenever there's a marriage or a funeral, a human or animal is ill, or there's any kind of problem in a family, the head of the family will go to the mountain to make offerings and pray for compassion. They offer yaks, sheep, and other goods to the stonecutter, who then chooses a rock for them from the mountain and carves into it the six syllables of the great mantra. These carvings use many different kinds of calligraphy and can be painted a multitude of colors. Some mani stones are engraved with whole paragraphs of Buddhist scripture, while others are carved with images of the Buddha.

"People don't take the mani stones away with

them. They are simply a symbol of their faith and bring them spiritual comfort. That is why you often see great piles of mani stones in among the mountain rocks we pass."

Wen listened carefully to Zhuoma's explanation.

"More and more I feel how faith informs everything in Tibet," she said. "Here, people place themselves entirely in the hands of heaven and nature. Even the mountains, waters, and plants speak of faith."

"It is true," said Zhuoma. "Even though, here in the north, life is very different from my family lands, where there are roads, agriculture, and more people, we Tibetans all have the same spirituality. Because we are isolated from the outside world, we believe that here all things between heaven and earth exist as they should. We believe that our own gods are the only gods and our own ancestors are the source of all life in the world. We are cut off from the march of time. When our farmers sow their seeds, they simply leave the fate of their crops to the heavens. There are no modern farming techniques. The farmers behave as their ancestors did hundreds or even thousands of years ago, as do the nomads. Both groups have a very difficult life. They are obliged to give away much of their crops and animals as offerings to the monasteries. This is a very heavy burden for people who have so little, but they must honor the lamas who protect them.

"People believe that the Dalai Lama of southern Tibet and the Panchen Lama of northern Tibet are the most senior human representatives of the spirits. When they die, a new reincarnation is sought through prayer and special rites: for example, khata scarves, precious bottles, and potions are thrown into a specially chosen lake, after which the surface of the water will reveal the map of the reincarnation's birthplace. Once selected, the new Dalai and Panchen Lamas live out the rest of their lives in magnificent palaces."

"It is so very different from China," said Wen. "For us, religion is not a strong force. We obey only lay rulers."

"But who controls and protects your rulers?" Zhuoma asked, puzzled.

"Conscience," replied Wen.

"What kind of thing is 'conscience'?"

"It is not a thing," said Wen. "It is a moral code."

"And what is a 'moral code'?"

Wen reflected. She suddenly realized that this was a very difficult question to answer. She thought of Kejun, a man who had to find an answer to all questions and then a reply to all the answers. Perhaps Tibet had changed him too.

By this time the two women had reached the lake and they stopped to set down their water casks.

Wen turned to Zhuoma. "I cannot forget my Kejun," she said.

Zhuoma nodded. "I, too, have been thinking of Tiananmen. I have seen that Gela's family has built up their stores. Perhaps now that summer is here, we can ask Gela for food and horses. I will try to speak to him."

## 5

When Zhuoma and Wen returned from the lake, they found two men in the tent, both carrying rifles with bayonets. Wen assumed that they must be relatives of Gela's family, or were perhaps known to Zhuoma because she immediately engaged them in conversation. The men received a warm welcome from the whole family, who cooked a great hunk of mutton in their honor, and the aroma of roasted meat and barley wine filled the tent.

Once the men had gone, Zhuoma told Wen that the men had been passing travelers who were gathering medicinal herbs. Neither she nor Gela knew them but, in Tibet, all travelers received an enthusiastic welcome because they were the bearers of news. It was traditional to treat them with great respect and offer the best food. Their horses would be checked over by the men while the women would prepare them water and dried provisions for their journey. Sadly, this group of men had not been able to offer much information that was of use, either to Gela or to Zhuoma and Wen.

Early the next morning, as the first rays of sun were scattering over the grassland, everyone set about their tasks as usual. The men started to herd the sheep and yaks toward the slopes of a mountain to the south. This was the only time during the day that the three men raised their voices. There was an undertone of excitement to their vigorous calls as they drove their beasts, and the sound mingled with the lowing and bleating of the animals. Zhuoma set off for the lake with Ni and Hum chattering and laughing behind her, as if the empty waterskins on their backs were filled with happiness. Saierbao, Pad, and Wen set about churning the butter, a skill that Wen had now mastered. She was full of new hope and confidence. Zhuoma was planning to offer Gela some of her jewelry in exchange for two horses, and although Wen had nothing to give, she had decided that she would leave behind her book of Liang Shiqiu's essays. For a while now, between the evening meal and prayers, the children had been asking her to read aloud a passage from the book, which Zhuoma would try to translate. It was difficult for her to understand Liang Shiqiu's philosophical writing, but it helped her improve her Chinese. Every day she and the children learned something new.

Suddenly, Wen saw Pad standing in a trance at the tent door, staring into the distance. When Saierbao called out to her to come and help with the butter, she didn't move. Even more strangely, she then walked twice around the tent. Although Saierbao seemed unperturbed by her daughter's behavior, Wen was puzzled. She walked over to the tent door and saw, in the distance, Ni and Hum running toward them. There was no sign of Zhuoma.

When the children finally reached the tent, they were in tears. Wen watched Saierbao turn pale as she listened to what they were telling her and then run out of the tent to wave and shout at the far-off figures of Gela, Ge'er, and Om. Wen waited anxiously for the men to arrive back at the tent so that she could find out what had happened. All she could understand from the children's babbling was the word "Zhuoma" repeated over and over again.

After what seemed like hours, the men entered the tent and listened to what the children had to say. Wen implored them in gestures to explain to her what was being said. It was Ge'er who, as so often, seemed to understand her. Taking a board that was usually used for working sheepskin, he threw some barley flour over it and drew a few pictures with his finger. Although crude, the pictures were clear enough. A group of men on horseback had thrown a sack over Zhuoma's head and carried her off. When Wen had recovered from her initial shock, she laboriously asked Ni if she had seen anything else. Ni pulled down the sleeve of her robe to reveal several long scratches on her right shoulder. Hum placed Wen's hand on his head, where she felt a large bump. She guessed they must have been hurt struggling with whoever had kidnapped Zhuoma. Wen had no idea why anyone would have wanted to take her. It was inconceivable. Unless they were some unknown enemies of Zhuoma's, or Chinese soldiers.

For the rest of the day, Wen asked Ni and Hum many questions using gestures, pictures, and objects in an attempt to find out some more details about what had happened. It seemed that while Zhouma and the children were on their way home with the water, the group of men had ridden up to them, lassoed Zhouma as they would a horse, and bundled her into a large cloth sack—the kind used to carry offerings. The children could understand what the men had been saying, so they must have been Tibetans. Two of them, it appeared, were the men who had visited their tent the day before. Ni told Wen that Zhuoma had continued to struggle, even after she'd been flung over the horse's back. Wen remembered Pad's strange behavior on the morning of the kidnapping. Had she seen or sensed something? She tried to ask her if she knew where Zhuoma was now, but Pad simply shook her head and pointed to her mouth, not saying a word. Wen had no idea what she meant.

In the days that followed, Gela and Ge'er spent hours scouring the surrounding land on horseback, looking for a sign of Zhuoma and her kidnappers, but they had melted into thin air. Each evening the men would return disconsolate. When they caught her eye, Wen understood that they had no hope of finding Zhuoma, and that they pitied Wen, who now found herself completely alone and unable to communicate.

AS SUMMER turned to autumn, Wen entered the darkest period of her life. At night, she would weep for the woman whose sleeping space now lay empty at her side, remembering her courage and intelligence. During the day, she struggled to manage without Zhuoma as an interpreter. The odd sentence of Tibetan that Zhuoma had managed to teach her—a few verbs and words like "yes" and "no"—allowed her to go about her daily tasks, but outside these routines, she was confined to a world of silence. And she had little hope of learning more Tibetan. Gela's family lived their lives in a kind of tacit understanding. Even when they had the time to talk to each other, it was rare to hear them in conversation. Without language, how would she ever be able to persuade them to help her leave their home and risk her life alone on the plateau? Aside from the fact that she had his photograph, the family knew nothing of Kejun. Zhuoma had advised her not to tell them that the Chinese army was in Tibet. They would not understand why and it would frighten them.

Would she ever be able to tell them that she loved her husband so much she was prepared to suffer anything to find him?

Wen was eaten up by pain and disappointment. It was as if she had drawn close to her husband only to see him disappear yet again. She was trapped and could see no way out.

AFTER ZHUOMA'S disappearance, the family seemed far more fearful. Ni's merry laughter dried up and the usually irrepressible Hum now clung silently to his mother instead of prancing and skipping around the tent. When the time came to move to their next pasture, Gela seemed to choose an even more remote place to settle. If they saw a human form in the distance, Gela would signal to his family to keep out of sight. Once or twice, he even hid Wen among the sheep so that she couldn't be seen by passing travelers, as if he was worried that she too might be carried off. It felt like they were leaving the world of men far behind them.

Wen began to keep a diary. Every day she would use one of her colored stones to write a few lines on one of the pages of *The Collected Essays of Liang Shiqiu.*

The stones left only a faint indentation. She had to condense and limit her writing in order to save paper. Nevertheless, the diary was her only means of recording her thoughts and retaining her ability to write Chinese. It gave her a new strength and determination to survive.

ONE MORNING, Ni fainted as she was helping Saierbao with the milking. Saierbao yelled out to her husbands for help, and Gela carried Ni back to the tent. Clearly troubled, Gela said something to Ge'er, who immediately left the tent and began to saddle his horse. Gela then mumbled a few words to Saierbao, who went over to the stove and put some water on to boil. Using all the Tibetan she had learned, Wen tried to tell Saierbao that she was a menba, that she might be able to help them, but Saierbao looked at her blankly and continued what she was doing. Suddenly, Hum cried out, pointing at Ni's lower body. Everyone's eyes followed his pointing finger: blood was seeping through Ni's robe. Gela told Pad to take Hum outside, then gestured at Wen to help him open Ni's clothing. On the garments under her robe they found layer upon layer of bloodstains.

Now Wen finally understood why Ni had been weeping every night: she must have been bleeding like this for ages. She remembered Zhuoma telling her that because fetching water was so backbreaking, the women were very skilled at saving on clothes washing and went to great lengths to avoid menstrual bloodstains. Ni's bleeding could not therefore be simply an ordinary period.

Trying to hold back her tears, Saierbao gestured to Wen that they had all known about this problem for a long time, but didn't know what to do.

Gela soaked a piece of felt in hot water, wrung it dry, spat a couple of mouthfuls of barley wine onto it, wrung it out again, and walked over to the statue of Buddha to pray. He then wrapped the piece of felt around Ni's feet and spat another mouthful of barley wine over her forehead. Ni's lips moved slightly and her eyes opened a crack. She looked toward her mother, who was turning her prayer wheel and praying in front of the altar. Gela called Saierbao over and placed their daughter's hand in hers. Ni gave a faint smile, then closed her eyes.

Wen stepped forward and took her pulse. It was terribly weak and she was continuing to lose blood. Yet without medical equipment or medicine, there was nothing Wen could do to help her. She was torn apart by guilt and frustration.

Throughout the day, the whole family kept a silent vigil by Ni's side; even Hum—so hungry that he was sucking his fingers—remained totally quiet. Saierbao and Gela knelt together in front of the Buddha, endlessly turning the prayer wheel while they prayed.

At dusk, the sound of galloping hooves signaled Ge'er's return. He had a bag in his hands, which the three adults quickly opened. They mixed its powdery contents with water and fed it to Ni. Wen watched, fascinated, but had no idea what they were giving her. Ten minutes later, Wen could see some color return to Ni's cheeks.

No one slept that night. Gela gestured at the exhausted Wen to rest. She lay down, listening to the turning of prayer wheels until daybreak.

THEY WERE unable to save the lovely, lively Ni. Her spirit had gone too far away. The day after her collapse, the young girl, who couldn't have been more than fourteen, lost her life.

Wen was overcome with grief. She mourned for the family, but also for herself. Of all the members of Gela's family, Ni was the one she had spent the most time with, and who had brought her the most happiness. Now she had lost both Zhuoma and Ni in quick succession. Her future stretched out before her in a hopeless abyss.

Wen was terrified that the family would give Ni a sky burial. Zhuoma had described how, after her father's death, his corpse had been cut into pieces and left on a mountain altar for the vultures to eat. She had answered Wen's disgust by saying that sky burial was merely another manifestation of the harmony in Tibet between heaven and earth, nature and man: there was nothing to be disgusted by. But, although Wen remembered Zhuoma's words, she didn't think she could bear to watch Ni's body being fed to vultures. In any event, she was spared: the family took the corpse to the lake for a water burial.

AUTUMN BECAME winter, winter became spring. Wen found that she could no longer keep track of the passing years. She simply followed the family as they moved in search of fresh pastures and shelter from the elements. To her, each mountain, each prairie looked the same; to them, there were subtle distinctions. As often as she could, she wrote in her book—letters to Kejun that she hoped she would one day deliver to him; details of her daily life. The words piled up. Once she had filled the blank pages in the book of essays, she started writing between the lines of text. Once those spaces were filled, she wrote over the faint imprints already there. The only space in which she would not write was the inside cover. She reserved this for Kejun. When she found him, he would write an epilogue to her diary. The pages overflowed with Wen's loneliness, her love, her will to survive.

The book became thicker and thicker.

Kejun's photograph yellowed. His face looked worn and wrinkled.

As there was no opportunity of escape, Wen

stopped thinking about escape. Her body and mind adapted to the Tibetan way of doing things; she ceased to be so aware of her needs and desires. When the family prayed, she joined them, spinning her own prayer wheel. She added to the prayers the words of Wang Liang: "Just staying alive is a victory."

The closest Wen came to having contact with the world beyond the family tent was the festival of Weisang. In the autumn, men would gather in huge numbers from all around the region to make offerings to the ancestors. Since women were not allowed to participate, Wen, Saierbao, Pad, and Hum would watch from the hillside as hundreds of horse riders carrying brightly colored flags moved in ritual formations around the sacrificial altar. Gela would bring back jewelry for Saierbao that joined the many ornaments with which she adorned herself. At first Wen didn't understand how this poor family could spend their money on luxuries instead of buying animals. As time went on, she realized that these ornaments were not considered to be material wealth but were in fact religious objects.

GELA, GE'ER, and Om could not attend Weisang every year but they went as often as they could. The first time Wen had seen them set off on their horses, she had been alarmed. The size of their packs indicated that they would be gone for some time and she couldn't understand why they were leaving the women and children alone. It was Pad who had tried to explain. She had imitated her father and drawn Wen a picture in barley flour showing three suns decorated with implements for breakfast, lunch, and supper. Under the middle sun, she drew three men. By this, Wen had understood that the men would arrive at their destination at midday and were not going too far away. But she was still very confused.

Two days later, Saierbao had told her children to change into their festival robes and had found a colorful silk sash to tie around Wen's waist. They had tethered the livestock to yak-hair ropes outside the tent, secured the door, and set out on their horses. Saierbao had issued very few instructions to her children as they prepared to leave and they had followed her without speaking. By now, Wen was familiar with this silent way of doing things and she found it less disconcerting.

After a three-hour ride, they had stopped to eat. Suddenly Hum had pointed ahead, laughing and shouting. In the distance was a sea of people and flags. The flags fluttering in the breeze mingled with the flapping of banners planted in the ground and everywhere was alive with color and movement. Smoke and the smell of burning wood from the sacred fire enveloped the scene in a shimmering haze. Wen thought she had been transported to another world. After so many months of privation and solitude, the crowds, color, and noise seemed like a vision.

As the years went by, Wen grew accustomed to such extraordinary manifestations of faith. She also grew accustomed to the lack of news of the outside world. The only change to her life that Weisang brought was a wife for Om in a marriage arranged between the two families at the festival. Om's wife, Maola, was very similar in temperament to Saierbao: a woman of few words, serene and hardworking, and always smiling. Although Om still played his lute outside the tent every night, his music was much happier than it had been.

Not long after the wedding, Maola became pregnant. Two young sheep were separated from the flock and tethered to the tent. Wen observed them being fattened up to serve as nourishment for Maola at the time of the birth and to celebrate the arrival of a new family member. It was when she watched in amazement as Gela and Ge'er skillfully delivered a healthy baby girl into the hands of Om that she realized her identity as a doctor, and indeed as a Chinese woman, was falling away from her.

That evening, Gela led his whole family in prayers for the newborn. Saierbao and Wen had been hard at work all day preparing the feast. At the banquet, Saierbao presented Wen with one of the crisp roasted legs of lamb. For as long as Wen could remember, that part of the lamb had always been reserved for Gela and Ge'er. Saierbao's gesture seemed to be saying to her, "You are one of us now. Share in our happiness."

6

*THE THIRTEEN HOLY MOUNTAINS*

Throughout the years that Wen spent with Gela's family, she clung to her belief that one day she would be reunited with Kejun. Although in many ways she had adopted the Buddhist way of life and, like the Tibetans around her, was accepting of her fate, a part of her would never renounce her quest. Her thoughts about Kejun were confined to her diary, but as her Tibetan improved and she found herself able to express herself with greater subtlety, she began to try to explain her feelings to the family. Hum was the first person she talked to about Kejun. The strong spirituality she had noticed in him when she first arrived had grown over the years and she felt able to confide in him. She remembered how, as a small boy, he had been so frightened of Kejun's photograph. Now she drew it out and showed it to him. "This man," she said, "is my beloved. My sun and my moon."

Gradually Kejun became part of the conversation. The family would listen spellbound as Wen told them about her former life in China. Pad in particular, now a grown woman, seemed to drink in information about this very different world in the east. Finally the day arrived that Wen had never dared hope for. Gela came to her and announced that the family had decided to help her in her search. Hum was now of an age to be of help to Gela and so Ge'er could be spared. Pad also wished to accompany them and Gela had agreed since her mysterious gift for prediction might be of use to Wen. He would give them three horses and sufficient dry provisions to keep them going for some time. When these ran out, they could rely on the generosity of other Tibetans and the monasteries.

When she heard how the family was planning to separate in order to help her, Wen wept. She didn't know what to say. There were no words sufficient to express her debt to them. Not only had they rescued her from death, they had made her a part of their loving family for many years. Seeing Wen's tears, Saierbao quietly took her hand and gently stroked it. Wen felt the roughness of Saierbao's skin. She had aged. Her colorful clothes had faded, her ornaments were tarnished, but her face still shone.

Their parting was a solemn affair. Gela and Saierbao watched silently as Ge'er loaded the horses. Saierbao had prepared sacks of food and waterskins; there was a tent, bedding, rope, and medicines.

As Hum held the bridle of Wen's horse for her to mount, he confided quietly to Wen that, as soon as Ge'er was back, he intended to enter a monastery as his brothers Ma and Me had done. He had reflected on Wen's words about Kejun: he thought he understood what her love was like because, for him, the spirits were as the sun and moon.

Amid all the farewells, Wen removed the carnelian necklace Zhuoma had given her and pressed it into Saierbao's hands, along with the old army uniform that she had never worn again. Images of Ni's face filled Wen's head. She knew that wherever she went, she would never forget the girl who had been like a beautiful wind chime, or the quiet love of her family.

DURING THEIR plans for the journey, Pad had suggested to Ge'er that they seek out the stonecutters who carved the mani stones on sacred mountains. These men were visited by all manner of people who wished to make an offering to the gods. Perhaps they would have news of any Chinese people who had passed that way in recent years. Ge'er agreed that this was how they should start.

For many months, their inquiries were fruitless. They traveled from mountain to mountain but none of the stonecutters that Ge'er talked to recognized Kejun's photograph or had met any Chinese. Nor was Wen able to glean any information about what had happened to the People's Liberation Army in this area of Tibet. "Is the conflict over?" she asked the people they met. They just looked at her strangely and did not reply.

Then, one day, they came across an old stonecutter who did recall having met some Chinese. Wen and Pad waited while Ge'er climbed the mountain to speak to him. When he returned, he reported excitedly that, many years ago, the stonecutter had seen a group of Tibetans pass by, among whom were some Chinese. They had all been wearing Tibetan robes but it had been easy to spot the non-Tibetan faces among them because they hadn't been burned bronze by the harsh plateau sun. Each of them carried a rifle with a bayonet. There was a wriggling bundle on one of the horses. He had assumed that there was a live animal inside. The men had said they were heading northeast.

Wen and Pad looked at Ge'er in astonishment. Could these men have been Zhuoma's kidnappers? Wen thought they should head northeast to see if they could gather more information, but Ge'er was anxious that they were abandoning the search for Kejun. Perhaps it would be better, he suggested, to travel toward the southeast, where, according to several of the people they had met, they would find many Chinese.

Wen gazed up into the deep blue sky, her hand on the photograph of Kejun in her breast pocket. "Zhuoma saved my life. We Chinese like to repay debts. I think if Kejun knew, he would want me to look for Zhuoma first."

THE ROAD northeast would take them through high, windswept mountain passes. Ge'er warned Wen that it was only possible to cross the snow-capped mountains in summer, so they would have to wait out the winter at their foot. They spent the winter months in their tent, building up their strength and energy. Ge'er hunted antelope and other wild animals and gathered edible plants. He showed Wen and Pad how to recognize the medici nal roots that still clung to life in freezing temperatures.

In the spring, they set off again, traveling for days in near silence, concentrating on guiding their horses safely through the difficult terrain. Shortly after they had finally descended from the mountain ridge, they encountered a group of pilgrims. They wore long pieces of felt on their fronts and wrapped around their hands and feet. Wen soon saw the reason for this. After every step forward, the pilgrims prostrated their entire bodies on the ground so that even their foreheads touched the earth. They got up and repeated the whole full-body obeisance. Seeing Wen and her companions, the pilgrims stopped to rest. They said that they had been traveling for four months on a pilgrimage to Mount Anyemaqen. Wen knew that Anyemaqen was several weeks' hard ride away. At the rate they were going, it would take them years. She wondered whether her own faith could sustain her in the same way.

AFTER THAT, they saw no one. Wen added another line to her diary, covering over words she had written many years earlier: "Help me, Kejun! I know you're watching me—wait for me!"

Just as their food and water were about to run

out, they spotted a tent. The three weary travelers were given a warm welcome by the nomad family and stayed with them for two days and nights. Wen could see that this family's living conditions were very different from those of Gela's family. They had plenty of semimechanized household and farming tools, a bicycle, and even a tractor. It had not occurred to her that the life of the Tibetan people could differ so much from place to place.

The head of the family explained that all these things had been bought from "truck shops" that had been traveling around this part of Tibet during the last few years.

"Are the shops run by the Chinese?" Wen asked.

"No, they are Tibetan merchants," the man replied.

Ge'er was amazed by all the machines, gingerly prodding them. He couldn't stop asking questions.

"What do these little iron things eat?"

"What do they do at night?"

"Do they ever get angry?"

"Can you ride a bicycle on the mountains?"

"How many pieces of dung can a tractor pull at once?"

Wen had never heard Ge'er talk so much.

. . .

BEFORE THEY set off again, their host asked them whether his son Zawang, who was also planning to go north, could travel with them. Ge'er was only too happy with this arrangement. An extra man in the party, and a young, strong one at that, would mean that the journey's chores—fetching water and firewood, lighting cooking fires, putting up the tent, mending harnesses and saddles—would become much lighter.

The presence of Zawang changed their mood and relieved the monotony of the journey. Pad seemed particularly delighted by him. Wen had never known her to talk and laugh so much. Watching the two young people together, she and Ge'er often looked at each other and smiled.

Zawang was on his way to the renowned monastery of Wendugongba to see his older brother, who was a lama there. He hadn't seen his brother for ten years because the monastery hadn't permitted family visits during that time. His brother had needed all his attention to concentrate on learning to sew the intricate tapestries that the monastery was famous for. Zawang explained that, for these tapestries, pieces of fabric were sewn onto a padded background to create elaborate and beautiful pictures of the spirits. His brother's work now hung upon the walls of the monastery. Wen was overcome by nostalgia for the embroidered clothes she had worn in the Yangtze delta—the padded silk jackets decorated with dragons and phoenixes in colored thread. She thought of her parents and her sister, who must, by now, believe that she was dead. She reached into her robe and touched the book that still contained her sister's paper crane.

WHEN THEY arrived at Wendugongba, Wen and Pad waited outside because women were not permitted within the precincts of the monastery. The lama who received the men told Zawang that his brother was absent from the monastery, accompanying the abbot on an administrative visit around the region. However, all travelers were welcome guests at the monastery and he and his companions could await his return at the monastery's guesthouse nearby.

The accommodation separated men and women. Wen and Pad were led to a simple mud-brick room, with an adjoining room for their animals. The doors and windows were made of oiled felt rugs nailed into wooden frames. The room was about fifteen meters square, the main wall hung with a long religious scroll. Beneath this were some simple wooden shelves. Two single beds were the only other furniture, except for two rush cushions on the floor for meditation and reading the scriptures.

Wen almost cried when she saw the room: it had been so long since she had slept somewhere with walls that she felt quite overwhelmed. She sat on the bed and savored the privacy it offered. To share a sleeping space with only one other woman was a huge luxury.

When she examined the few objects on the wooden shelves, she was astonished to find that several of them came from China. There was a plastic bag from the famous Rongbaozhai art-materials shop in Beijing and glazed paper made in Chengdu; there was even a torch made in Shanghai. Seeing these things brought more tears to her eyes: other than her own meager belongings, she hadn't seen a single object with a Chinese connection for years. Chinese people must have brought their possessions to this empty room. She sensed she was drawing closer to the answer she sought.

At suppertime, a lama told them that a huge ceremony called the Dharmaraja would take place at the monastery in a few days' time. The lamas would be practicing in the open courtyard in front of the entrance to the monastery and their rehearsals must not be disturbed. The three Tibetans felt blessed that such an important religious festival would be taking place while they were at the monastery. Pad explained to Wen that whoever had their head touched by the Dharmaraja would attain peace, safety, and their heart's desire.

THAT EVENING, before the men and women separated to go to their separate quarters, Wen asked Ge'er if it would be possible to make inquiries about Kejun the next day at the monastery. Ge'er promised to talk to the lamas in the morning.

Before she fell asleep, Wen inlaid yet another line of text in her book: "Jun, today I have seen Chinese writing again. This must be a sign from you. My dearest husband, tonight please tell me in my dreams where you are." But Wen lay awake all night, unvisited by dreams.

The next day, a lama came especially to let Wen know that they would inform the whole monastery of her search at the hour for scripture debate, and that they would also ask the visitors and sightseers who attended the forthcoming Dharmaraja festival.

AT DAWN on the day of the ceremony, several large gongs rang, waking Wen. Looking out of her window, she saw a figure standing silhouetted on the roof of the monastery: a lama dressed in a purple robe, banging a huge bronze gong. For the next two hours, the lamas could be heard chanting the scriptures, the sound rising and falling through the buildings. Wen thought of Saierbao, Zhuoma, and Ni, three pious women who had spent their lives praying and reciting the scriptures.

Just before the ceremony was about to begin, a boy lama came running over to the guesthouse to escort them to the monastery's courtyard, situated in front of the ornate entrance to the monastery. He arranged for them to sit on the ground in the front row, which was the best position from which to receive the Dharmaraja's blessing.

This was the first time Wen had watched a Tibetan religious ceremony from such close range. She stared, entranced, at the sea of banners. In front of the monastery doors, eight long horns were propped up, flanked by lamas wearing tall, crested helmets. Lamas in costume were forming themselves into a great square. Suddenly, a line of lamas dressed in robes of red and gold sounded their glittering trumpets. A group of performers, looking rather like Peking Opera actors, came striding out of the monastery building. "These are the lamas who are going to perform the dance," Pad whispered to Wen. "When the Dharmaraja passes, don't forget to step forward with me so he can touch your head."

It was an incredible spectacle. Dozens of dancers, dressed in bright colors and wearing headdresses that represented horses or cattle, filled the court-yard. Lamas chanted sutras and blew on copper horns and conch shells. Blasts from the longer horns set the pace of the dance, as the Dharmaraja went around the spectators bestowing blessings. Wen had no idea what the dance meant, but she was exhilarated by what she saw.

She turned to survey the crowd to see if the other spectators were similarly uplifted by watching this extraordinary communion between the human and spirit worlds. To her astonishment, she noticed a number of Chinese faces. Her heart missed a beat to see the familiar blue, black, and gray of their cloth-ing among the brightly colored Tibetan clothes. Although her instinct told her to push her way through the throng toward them, she was overcome by the gulf that now separated her from the world she had left. She had not uttered a Chinese word out loud for many years. Would she even be able to speak to them?

She made her way cautiously through the sea of people, trying to find a group of Chinese people who looked approachable. When she spotted a woman of about her own age, animatedly discussing the ceremony with her friends, she went up to her and bowed her head.

"Excuse me," she said. "Can I ask you a question?"

The words felt strange in her mouth.

"You speak Chinese?" the woman asked, clearly surprised that someone who looked like a Tibetan nomad could speak her language.

"I am Chinese," Wen said sadly. "But I have been in Tibet since 1958."

How could she possibly begin to explain what had happened to her?

The woman and her friends were amazed. They overwhelmed her with a torrent of questions.

"How did you get here? Were you a prisoner?"

"When did you learn to speak Tibetan?"

"Do you live with Tibetans? How do they treat you?"

"Is your family here?"

One of the men in the group suggested that they find a quiet place to talk, away from the crowds.

"We have many things to ask you," he said, "but I sense that you also have questions that you want to ask. Let's go and sit on that hillside over there."

. . .

THE SMALL group of people assembled themselves in a circle on the hillside. Besides the man, who Wen learned was originally from Hubei and worked in agriculture, there was a young man and woman from Henan who worked as technicians in a Tibetan hospital and an older woman from Sichuan who was a teacher. They all had different reasons for coming to live in Tibet. The young people told her that they had taken advantage of the financial incentives offered by the Chinese government to move to Tibet; there were many jobs to be found here. The older man said he had come to Tibet in the 1970s when agricultural workers from Hubei were in demand because it was preferable to the difficult political situation in China. The woman said that, because Sichuan was close to the Tibetan border, she had moved to Tibet in the 1960s to "support the border regions."

It took some time for Wen to explain to them how she came to be dressed in Tibetan clothing, her face weather-beaten, her hands rough. When she had finished, the group was utterly silent. They looked at her in disbelief.

It was the older woman who broke the silence.

"You know, don't you, that the fighting between the Chinese and Tibetans ended long ago?" she asked.

Wen didn't reply, although her mind was reeling from this information. There seemed no way to communicate to these people the kind of isolated life she had experienced. They knew next to nothing about the empty plains of Qinghai or the nomadic way of life. Though they lived in Tibet, they remained enclosed in their Chinese communities. How could she tell them that she had been living in a place where there were no politics, no war, only the calm self-sufficiency of a communal life where everything was shared—and limitless space, where time stretched out endlessly.

"Please tell me," she asked, "what is the situation now between the Chinese and the Tibetans?"

The woman and her friends looked at each other.

"In the time you have been in Tibet," the woman said, "China has changed greatly. Perhaps more than you can guess. It is difficult for us to know exactly what is happening in Tibet and why the Dalai Lama is no longer here."

Since her conversations with Zhuoma all those years ago, Wen had not given much thought to the Dalai Lama, but she was nevertheless shocked to learn that he wasn't living in the Potala Palace as she had imagined.

"But why did he leave?" she asked.

"I don't know," said the woman. "I've heard people say that relations between the Chinese government and the Dalai Lama were pretty good to begin with—and that, in the early 1950s, the Communist government had the support of the Tibetan people and the approval of the Tibetan elite. Otherwise, why would the Dalai Lama, who had gone into hiding in the tiny remote border village of Yadong, have returned to the capital, Lhasa? And why would he have sent representatives to Beijing in 1951 to sign the Communist government's Agreement for the Peaceful Liberation of Tibet, making Tibet an autonomous region of China? Apparently the Dalai Lama's meeting with Chairman Mao Tse-tung in 1954 was very friendly and the Dalai Lama was impressed by Mao's intelligence and ability. The poem he wrote in praise of Chairman Mao and the Golden Wheel of a Thousand Blessings, which he presented to Beijing, are said to be proof of this. In that year, both he and the Panchen Lama accepted the mandate of the Chinese government at the National People's Congress, which showed that Tibet endorsed the Beijing regime."

"Some people say that," the older man interrupted, "but others believe the Dalai Lama was young and impressionable. The Beijing government brainwashed him. But, although they might have managed to influence his emotions over minor issues, they could never have made him relinquish his belief in Tibet's independence. People may say that in the early 1950s Mao had no intention of using force in Tibet and that he knew better than to interfere with the way the Tibetans governed themselves, but would he have tolerated an independent Tibet? It is easy to understand why he sent in the army in 1958. There was unrest in the southwest of China and Chiang Kai-shek had announced that he was building up his forces in Taiwan to launch an attack on the Communists. It was essential that Mao had Tibet under his control. The only reason he had been so easy on Tibet after 1949 was because the Korean War had diverted the manpower and resources of the Liberation Army elsewhere. But by the end of the 1950s, the Liberation Army had had a few years to recover its strength and was ready to deal with Tibet. The Dalai Lama was accepting weapons from the West and giving tacit support to the Tibetan Independence Movement. Mao had no choice but to send in the army."

The woman spoke again. "Who can know the truth? The Dalai Lama was torn in half. On the one hand, the Chinese government's promise to allow Tibet to opt out of their reform movement was being broken. Political campaigns such as 'Kill the rich, help the poor,' 'Universal equality,' and 'Zero tolerance of religion' were undermining the authority of Tibet's feudal overlords, and shaking the Dalai Lama's trust in Beijing. On the other hand, he did not want to anger Beijing. So he tried to play both games: he took an active role in the political projects initiated by the Chinese government while turning a blind eye to the Tibetan Independence Movement's efforts to stir up military rebellion through the Army of Defenders of the Faith. But he was like a man standing in two boats at the same time: he ended up with nothing. Beijing sent its soldiers to destroy the age-old unity of church and state in Tibet, while the Army of Defenders of the Faith, despite Western support, was unable to protect the Dalai Lama's throne. In his haste to flee, the Dalai Lama didn't even dare wear his own clothes. He'd been told by reliable sources that the Liberation Army in Tibet was planning to take him prisoner as punishment for trying to break with China. That was why so many Tibetans kept guard around the Potala Palace, to protect their spiritual leader—the incident that Beijing blamed as the 'trigger' that set off the unrest."

The young man and woman in the group had been very silent up to this point. Now the young man asked, "But if the Dalai Lama's flight was so sudden, why were there so many rumors about the treasure from the Potala Palace being taken out of the country one or two years before all this blew up, and how come the Dalai Lama has had all his treasure with him in exile? The late Chinese premier Zhou Enlai said that there was a godlike aspect to the Dalai Lama when he lived in the Potala Palace, but when a god leaves his temple, his air of holiness is tarnished. I think that now the Dalai Lama is no longer in Tibet, he has given up his struggle for independence."

"I am not sure that you are right," the older woman said. "I think he longs to return. Because of his efforts more and more people in the outside world are starting to take notice of Tibet. The government tells us that they have tried many times to hold a dialogue with the Dalai Lama, but he has always refused any contact. Many Tibetan people I talk to tell me the opposite. What should we believe?"

She turned to Wen with a sad smile.

Wen's head was reeling. Never before had she heard a political conversation like this one. When she was young, she had been inspired by political ideals, but she and her friends had all believed the same thing. She wasn't sure she would ever untangle all the confusing information she had just been given. The truth, she thought, would always remain elusive because humans could never recover the past as it had actually happened.

It was getting late as the group walked down the hillside. Far more important to Wen than knowing about politics was finding her husband. Before she separated from these people, she was determined to find out if they could help her. But none of them had much practical advice to offer. They themselves, they said, had difficulty receiving letters from China.

"Perhaps if you go to Lhasa," the woman said, "the army officials there will have more information, or help you go back to China."

Wen thanked her. Although she longed with all her heart to return to Suzhou and to fold her parents and her sister in her arms, she knew that until she had some news of Kejun and Zhuoma she could not leave Tibet. She then watched the first Chinese people she had met in many years walk away from her. For a moment, she was tempted to run after them, but she stopped herself. She did not belong with them now. Ge'er and Pad were her family.

WHEN SHE returned to her room at the guesthouse, she found a lama sitting outside the door on the ground, telling his prayer beads. When he saw her, he looked up.

"I am told you are looking for a woman named Zhuoma."

"Yes," said Wen with excitement. "Do you know something?"

"I too am looking for her," said the lama. "Many years ago, I was her servant. We were separated while traveling in a storm. I wandered for days in search of her and would have died if a lama from this monastery who was gathering medicinal herbs in the mountains hadn't found me and carried me back here. I have devoted my life to this monastery since then, but I have never ceased to ask all visitors for news of my dear mistress."

Wen could barely speak. "You are Tiananmen," she said.

The lama was taken aback. "Yes," he said, "She named me Tiananmen."

IN THE days that followed the Dharmaraja ceremony, Tiananmen would visit Wen, Ge'er, and Pad in the intervals between scripture readings in the monastery's great hall. When he heard Zhuoma's story, he wrung his large hands until the joints cracked. After that he seemed preoccupied. He told them that he had petitioned the abbot for a period of leave from the monastery. He wished to join them in their search for Zhuoma. Sometime later, he came to them with the good news that his petition had been granted. What was more, the abbot was willing to give a blessing to their quest, in which were joined the fates of both Tibetans and Chinese. Tiananmen led them into the presence of the head lama, who listened patiently to their petition.

"On the high plateau," he said, "the sky may change, people may change, yaks and sheep, flowers and grasses all may change, but not the holy mountains. If you leave messages on the thirteen holy mountains, those with knowledge of Zhuoma will find them. Life starts in nature and returns to nature."

He gave Wen half a lead pencil, which, he told her, was a modern treasure belonging to the monastery. Wen was delighted. To her, too, this pencil was priceless: writing her diary had become her main consolation and her colored stone etched out no more than faint traces on the pages of her book. That evening, she wrote in clear black lines.

Only Pad seemed sad that they were leaving the monastery. Now that Zawang's brother had returned to the monastery with the head lama, Zawang was spending less time in her company. Whenever the lamas were released from their daily duties, Zawang would run off to talk to the brother he hadn't seen for ten years. How would Pad survive, Wen wondered, when she had been used to such companionship? But her worries were unnecessary. The day before they were due to leave, Ge'er came to her and told her that Zawang wished to accompany them on their journey. It seemed that he, too, could not bear to be parted from Pad. Horse messengers were sent to Gela and to Zawang's family to inform them about the discovery of Tiananmen, and of Zawang's decision to join the quest. They had sent such messengers before, but had never received back any news of Gela's family. Wen hoped that these messages would find their destination.

The monastery saw to their horses and their provisions. As they were climbing onto their horses, Wen noticed that Tiananmen had loaded his saddle with silk scrolls. She assumed that, as a lama, he needed to carry the scriptures with him. Once they were under way, however, Tiananmen explained that they were in fact messages asking for information about the lost Zhuoma. The monastery had taught him many things, including how to write. He told her about the scripture debates, where lamas came together to discuss interpretations of the scriptures in a formal group with a very particular set of rules. Wen felt herself growing closer to the taciturn Tiananmen with this rare glimpse into his world.

HOW MUCH time passed in that trek around the holy mountains of Qinghai? Wen lost track of the days and weeks. Her little group plodded onward, dogged in their determination to find Zhuoma, undaunted by the distances they covered and the hardship they suffered. Between each of the giant holy mountains lay other mountain ranges that they must cross. But they refused to give up: they would not stop until they had left Tiananmen's scrolls on all thirteen mountains.

Somewhere between the first and the third mountain, Ge'er gave his consent for Pad and Zawang to be married. The silent mountains were their witness. "We live under the eyes of the spirits," Ge'er told her. "This union is part of the divine plan." Wen wondered if Pad, with her gift for prediction, had always known something about this marriage. Perhaps this was why she had waited so long, in clear defiance of the Tibetan custom of early marriage, to join herself to someone. Would the spirits also guide Wen along her path? She felt their presence in her life more and more.

At the fifth mountain, Pad gave birth to a daughter and named her Zhuoma.

Wen worried about the addition of a baby to their group. The constant traveling was putting an intolerable strain on Pad and it did not seem right that Pad should be jeopardizing both her life and that of the child by continuing with the quest. Wen discussed her concerns with Tiananmen and Ge'er, and it was agreed that Ge'er should accompany Pad and Zawang to a place where they could build a proper life for their family. He would then return home to Gela and Saierbao: he had been away from his brother and wife for too long and it was time that he rejoined them. Tiananmen could protect Wen. Tiananmen suggested to Ge'er that he take the young couple to the southeast. He had heard at the monastery that, in this region, Chinese and Tibetans lived together. Pad and Zawang would find work, and their daughter could go to school.

As Wen watched Ge'er's horse recede into the distance, followed by Pad and Zawang, she wondered if she would ever see them again. The rest of her life would not give her enough time to repay all that Ge'er and his family had done for her. "Om mani padme hum," she murmured under her breath as the figures disappeared into the mountains.

・ ・ ・

IT WAS at the ninth mountain that they found Zhuoma's message. The mountain was covered with pile upon pile of mani stones inscribed with the mantra and passages of Buddhist scripture.

"They are the Diamond Sutra," said Tiananmen. "There is one chapter of scripture to each cairn."

"May I touch them?" Wen asked.

"You may," replied Tiananmen. "When you place your fingers on the words, you will feel the presence of the spirits."

For a while the two of them separated, walking around the cairns, reading the prayers preserved in stone. As Wen gazed at them, she tried in vain to imagine how many generations of hands had carved those holy words, piling them up on this mountain to be preserved for thousands of years. Suddenly Tiananmen called out. Wen turned. He was standing waving a white khata scarf that he had taken down from the line of prayer flags fluttering in the wind, and was shouting something indistinguishable. When she reached him, picking her way down the path, he was almost too overcome to speak. She took the scarf from his hands. On it was written a simple message: "Zhuoma is looking for Tiananmen. She awaits him at the next mountain, close to the stonecutter's hut."

Their hearts were in their mouths as they pushed their horses toward the neighboring mountain. How long had the message been there? Would Zhuoma have waited? It took them many days. When they arrived at the foot of the mountain, they saw in the distance a stonecutter's hut and, standing above it, the statuesque figure of a woman. As their horses thundered toward her, she turned. It was Zhuoma.

For a long time the three of them remained silent. No words could express the intensity of the emotions they felt. Wen got down from her horse and embraced the friend she had not seen for more than twenty years. Behind her, Tiananmen greeted his old mistress with quiet tears. He had found her, but could not hold her in his arms. In Tibet a single woman could not so much as touch the hand of a man whose life was pledged to the Buddha.

IT WAS evident from Zhuoma's silence on the subject that she did not wish to discuss what had happened to her since her kidnapping. Wen and Tiananmen would not have dreamed of undermining her dignity by asking. They learned only that she had been taken to the Chinese city of Xining, in the northeast corner of Qinghai, and had spent many years there before she found a way to leave. For two years she had searched for Gela's family. When she finally found them, Wen had long since left.

"How had you come to think of leaving messages in the holy mountains?" asked Wen, astonished that fate should have led Zhuoma to the same course of action as herself.

"A mani stonecutter told me something that I couldn't forget," replied Zhuoma. "He said, 'Tibetans always find what they have lost in the holy mountains.' I decided that, each year, I would visit all the holy mountains and if by winter I had received no news, I would return to the first mountain in spring and begin all over again. And that is what I have done," she said, looking sadly at Tiananmen. "I have visited each mountain many times and now the mountains have delivered to me what I had lost."

She turned to Wen.

"Have you found your Kejun?"

Wen could only shake her head.

"Then," said Zhuoma, "I want to help you find what you have lost. Please tell me what I should do."

Zhuoma's words felt to Wen like a gift from the heavens. Ever since she had met the Chinese people at Wendugongba, she had been reflecting on what she had learned about the Chinese presence in Tibet.

"I would like to go to Lhasa," she said. "I think that there I will find members of the Chinese army. It is possible that they might have some record of what happened to my husband's regiment."

Zhuoma glanced inquiringly at Tiananmen.

"I will take you both to Lhasa," he said, "but after that, I will be obliged to return to the monastery."

Wen could barely look at Zhuoma. She was overwhelmed by the painful realization that her friend would have to face once more the loss of the man she loved.

## 7

## OLD HERMIT QIANGBA

Wen, Zhuoma, and Tiananmen trekked south. It was summer when they reached the area known as the Hundred Lakes and saw the vast Zhaling lake stretching out like a sea beneath Mount Anyemaqen. The wind was gentle and the sun infused them with a sense of warmth and well-being. As they approached the water, they were surprised to see a great many tents down by the shoreline. Wen knew that gatherings were rare among the nomads. Some major celebration must have called these people here. It was in the summer months, when the yaks and sheep were fat, that Tibetans were able to be more sociable.

They pitched their own tent and tethered the horses. That evening, Tiananmen wandered around the other tents to barter for food with one of the ornaments that Zhuoma had clung to all these years. When he returned he said he had heard that a performance of a horseback opera would take place in two days' time. Wen was intrigued by the notion of an opera on horseback. Zhuoma remembered such performances from her childhood. They were acted by specially trained lamas, she explained, who rode in costume on horses. There was no talking or singing: it was the patterns that the men made as they rode to the music that told the story.

That night, although bone weary from the journey, Wen couldn't get to sleep. She was troubled by the faint sound of someone singing in the distance. It was a song unlike any she had heard before. She wondered if perhaps she was imagining it: Zhuoma and Tiananmen slept on undisturbed.

The next morning, when Wen told Zhuoma about the night singing, Zhuoma said the old people claimed that ghostly voices came from mountains. A little shiver ran down Wen's spine.

The two women had decided to spend the day exploring the lake on horseback and they set off early, taking a leather waterskin with them. As they rode eastward along the water's edge, they watched birds foraging and playing. A few thin clouds were scudding in the pure blue sky and swooping birds united the heavens and the earth. The scene reminded Wen of the Yangtze delta: of the river that flowed through her hometown, and of lakes Dongting and Tai, with their bobbing boats and little bridges made of stone and wood. Half lost in her thoughts, she told Zhuoma about a day when she and Kejun had raced paper boats on Lake Tai. Wen's boat, it turned out, had sailed smoothly off into the center of the lake, while Kejun's had just kept turning on the spot. How strange that, in Tibet, the tiny square of paper necessary to make a paper boat would cost more than a meal.

Zhuoma pulled on her reins. "Can you hear someone singing?"

Once the clop of their horses' hooves had stopped, the sound floated over very clearly: there really was a voice, a man's voice singing a sad melody. Zhuoma spotted two girls nearby carrying water and guided her horse over toward them.

"Can you hear that singing?" she asked.

The girls nodded.

"Do you know who it is?"

The older of the two girls pointed to a tiny dot on the other side of the lake.

"It's Old Hermit Qiangba," she said. "He sings there every day. I hear him whenever I go to fetch water. My mother says he is the guardian spirit of the lake."

The two women turned their horses to ride closer to the singer, but although they rode for two hours, the lake was so large that the hermit still seemed very far away. They could see nothing of his face, only his tattered garments fluttering in the wind. From a distance the large rock upon which he sat appeared to be floating in the middle of the water. When they drew nearer, they saw that it was at the end of a small spit of land that protruded into the lake.

"What is he singing?" Wen asked Zhuoma.

"It sounds as if it is part of the great legend of King Gesar," said Zhuoma. "The same story that will be performed at the horseback opera tomorrow. The legend has been passed down through the ages from storyteller to storyteller. It is the longest story in the world. Although people know it throughout Tibet, it is particularly dear to the people of this region because it is here, at the source of the Yellow River, that King Gesar made his kingdom."

Zhuoma thought that it might be easier to reach the hermit from the other side of the lake and suggested that they try again another day. As they retraced their steps, she told Wen a little about King Gesar.

Gesar was born into the ruling family of the ancient kingdom of Ling. He was a child of unusual bravery and resourcefulness. But when he became old enough to be king, his uncle Trothung, who wanted the throne for himself, sent Gesar and his mother into exile in a valley at the source of the Yellow River. The valley was a dark, freezing wilderness where neither sun nor moon shone, and it was plagued by demons. Gesar and his mother tamed the evil spirits and subdued the demons, brought order to the waters and grasses, and turned the valley into a fertile paradise for herders, where lush meadows teemed with yaks, horses, and sheep. The heavens later sent down blizzards and frosts to punish Trothung, making the kingdom of Ling uninhabitable. The people of Ling petitioned Gesar to let them come to him, and he gladly helped the six tribes of Ling settle at the source of the Yellow River. For this reason, all Tibetans who lived in this valley regarded themselves as the descendants of the kingdom of Ling—and the children of Gesar.

By the time the two women returned to their tent, Tiananmen had built a stove out of large stones, on top of which was sitting a pot giving off a delicious smell of meat. He told Zhuoma that he had got hold of half a sheep and had cooked it in the Chinese style.

"How did you learn to cook Chinese food?" asked Zhuoma in surprise.

"From you," Tiananmen replied. "You told me how, when you came back from Beijing."

"That's impossible," said Zhuoma. "I didn't even know how to make tsampa then, let alone Chinese food."

Tiananmen smiled. "But you talked to me about the Chinese dishes you ate in Beijing, and the taste of their stewed lamb. My father used to say, if you smell a horse's dung, you can tell where it's been grazing. If you taste barley wine, you can tell what the barley harvest was like. Didn't you tell me that the Chinese cook mutton with sweet herbs, that it is tender and comes in a salty broth? So that is how I have made it."

Both Zhuoma and Wen burst out laughing.

"You told me that he never asked questions," Wen said to Zhuoma. "But he was certainly listening."

Tiananmen's mutton was delicious. Wen couldn't recall having eaten anything flavored with those particular herbs, but she didn't say so. She never found out exactly what he had used.

During the meal, Tiananmen said he had heard that more than a thousand people would come to watch the horseback opera the next day. They could use the opportunity to make inquiries about Wen's husband. The three friends spent the evening in high spirits, as if sure that all their hopes would soon be realized. Wen went to sleep thinking of Kejun. Perhaps she would not need to travel to Lhasa. Perhaps the holy mountains would, after all, return to her what she had lost. In the night, the sound of the hermit singing drifted into her dreams. She and Kejun were following a great master, who was choosing mani stones for them on one of the holy mountains . . .

THE NEXT morning, crowds of people began to assemble on the hillside. Since the performance would take place on the plain, the slopes gave them a clear view of the action. Wen had seen nothing like this since the Dharmaraja ceremony at Wendugongba. She felt both fear and elation at the sight of so many people. She, Zhuoma, and Tiananmen arrived early, while the lamas were still painting their faces and preparing their costumes. Through the flaps in the actors' tents they could make out many of the beautifully colored props. A few young men hung around the tents, trying on hats, helmets, and garlands. Other young people were dancing, singing, and waving colored flags. There was an atmosphere of high excitement.

With the sounding of a few notes on a simple stringed instrument, the performance began. Wen had been worried that she wouldn't understand what was happening, but the stylized movements of the horseback actors made everything clear. The opera told the part of the legend where Gesar was sent down to earth by the bodhisattva Chenresig, who watched over the human world to rid mankind of evil spirits and demons, subdue all violence, and help the weak. The guardian spirit of the faith and the spirit of war accompanied Gesar into the world of men. Gesar won the horse race by which the ruler of the kingdom of Ling was chosen, and was given the title King Gesar and King of the Martial Spirits. Leading all the spirits, Gesar embarked on a military quest throughout the land, bringing peace and stability to the nation. This great task accomplished, the spirits flew back to the courts of heaven.

Wen thought the lamas looked like characters from the Peking Opera she had watched as a child in the teahouses of Nanjing, except they were mounted on horseback. Waving flags and banners, they rode out in various poses, producing strange shouts and roars. It all reminded Wen of the episode in *The Journey to the West* where Monkey King created havoc in heaven. Zhuoma stood at her side, quietly explaining the few parts that Wen couldn't understand.

"This is the fight with the demon king."

"That's the king's beautiful concubine praying for him."

"That villain is his uncle Trothung, gloating from the sidelines."

As she watched, Wen was full of admiration for the way in which the gestures of the actors were based on those of daily life. She was surprised that the actor-lamas, who lived enclosed in monasteries, could know these gestures so well. But perhaps there was not so much difference between the inside and the outside of a monastery. Increasingly, she was coming to understand that the whole of Tibet was one great monastery. Everyone was infused with the same religious spirit, whether they wore religious robes or not.

When evening came and the lamas had tethered their horses and packed up their costumes, the audience settled down around campfires, drinking barley wine and butter tea. Sheep were roasted whole over the bonfires and the smell wafted through the air as the fat spat and sizzled in the fire like fireworks.

Suddenly, there was a loud commotion and everyone rushed over to see what was going on. Someone called out for hot water and a menba.

Zhuoma squeezed into the crowd to listen to what was being said.

"A woman has gone into labor," she told Wen. "It sounds as if she's in trouble and her family is begging for help. Can you do anything?"

Wen hesitated. In all the years she had been in Tibet, she had hardly used her medical knowledge. The language barrier, the use of different herbs, the fact that Tibetans often relied on prayer when someone was seriously ill had rendered her hard-won knowledge useless. Would it be responsible for her now to claim she could help a difficult labor? Zhuoma saw her indecision.

"Come," she said. "They are desperate. At least go and see."

In a sparsely furnished tent lay a woman with an ashen face. Her whole body was shaking and streaked with blood. The baby's head was showing, but the rest couldn't emerge because the umbilical cord was wrapped around the neck. More dangerous still, the woman's family was urging her to bear down and the baby was turning purple, strangled by the tightening umbilical cord.

Wen cried out to the woman that she should stop pushing. As she washed her hands, she yelled instructions at Zhuoma on how to assist her. Silenced and impressed by her decisiveness, the family just stood by and watched.

Wen carefully pushed the baby's head back inside

the mother's body. She heard several sharp intakes of breath close by and she tried her hardest to remember the midwifery she had learned at medical school. For difficulties such as this, she needed gently to massage the womb. Zhuoma told everyone that she was a Chinese menba, that she was using Chinese methods of delivery to help them. Wen then gestured at the mother to push, and after a little while the baby emerged, slowly but surely. It was a healthy boy.

Surrounded by cries of excitement, Wen expertly cut the umbilical cord, drew out the afterbirth, and cleaned the woman's lower body with a special medicinal wine that the family brought to her. Then she watched as, like the children of Om and Pad, the baby was given a special herbal broth to protect it from insect bites.

When Wen passed the father the swaddled child, he was afraid to hold him. Instead, he opened his robe and asked Wen to put the child inside for him. He was overcome with emotion. He told Wen and Zhuoma that they had longed for a child for many years, but their hopes had been dashed every time because of miscarriages or problems in labor.

"Now I know of a second Chinese menba who has done a good thing," the man said.

Wen froze. "What do you mean?" she asked. "Have you met another Chinese doctor?"

"My father told me about one," the man replied. "He said that, many years ago, a Chinese doctor was given a sky burial and, because of this, the fighting between Tibetans and Chinese in this area came to an end."

Wen looked at Zhuoma. Her heart was pounding and she could hardly breathe.

Could this doctor have been Kejun?

Seeing her emotion, Zhuoma helped her to sit down.

"I don't know the details," the man continued, "but my father used to say that Old Hermit Qiangba knew the story."

At that moment, a man dashed into the tent and presented Wen with a snow-white khata scarf, a token of gratitude. Then he led her outside to the waiting crowd, who greeted her with whistles and cheers. Two old women, who were cooking mutton on a bonfire, came over and served her two fat legs of meat in honor of what she had done. The feasting went on well into the night. It was not until several hours later that Wen was able to return to her tent. She and Zhuoma had decided that first thing in the morning they would set out in search of Qiangba. She lay down, her head spinning slightly from the barley wine she had drunk. As the wind blew outside and the butter lamps flickered, she strained to hear the sound of singing from the lake.

THE DAY following the opera was to be given over to horse racing, but Wen and Zhuoma were oblivious to the excitement and commotion of the preparations as they made their way toward the lake. As they approached the place where they had seen the hermit, Wen was filled with anticipation. But to her dismay the stone where the hermit had sat was empty and none of the people drawing water at the lakeside knew where he had gone. The two women rushed back to ask the crowds watching the horse races, but no one there knew anything either. They waited the whole day at the lakeside but the hermit didn't return. The mysterious singer had vanished, taking his story with him.

Everyone they spoke to was sure he would be back: he was the guardian spirit of the lake. But for Wen, yet another hope had evaporated and the disappointment was almost too much to bear. Feeling as if she were on the verge of madness, she broke away from the others and galloped wildly around the lake, shouting the names of Kejun and Qiangba into the wind.

For several days, Wen did not speak. Zhuoma tried to console her by telling her that they were bound to find someone else who knew more about the local legend of the Chinese menba, but Wen was unable to answer. It was as if the endless succession of blows and disappointments had robbed her of all her powers of expression.

It was Tiananmen who roused her. Early one morning, he and Zhuoma saddled the horses and encouraged Wen to join them on a ride to a nearby mountainside.

"I would like to take you to see a sky burial site," said Tiananmen quietly.

A SKY burial had just taken place when the three friends arrived on the mountaintop. White khata scarves and streamers were fluttering in the breeze; little scraps of paper money danced and turned on the ground like snowflakes. They found themselves in a large gated enclosure in the center of which was a sunken area paved with stone. There was a walkway flanked by two stone altars.

As they stood talking, a man walked up to them and introduced himself as the sky burial master. He asked if he could help. Tiananmen stepped forward and bowed.

"We would like to learn about sky burial," he said.

Although the sky burial master looked a little surprised to be asked such a thing, he was not unwilling to grant their request.

"Humans are part of nature," he began. "We arrive in the world naturally and we leave it naturally. Life and death are part of a wheel of reincarnation. Death is not to be feared. We look forward eagerly to our next life. When a smoking fire of mulberry branches is lit in a sky burial site, it rolls out a five-colored road between heaven and earth, which entices the spirits down to the altar. The corpse becomes an offering to the spirits and we call upon them to carry the soul up to heaven. The mulberry smoke draws down eagles, vultures, and other sacred scavengers, who feed upon the corpse. This is done in imitation of the Buddha Sakyamuni, who sacrificed himself to feed the tigers."

Wen quietly asked the master to explain in detail how the corpse was laid out for the vultures.

"First the body is washed," he said, "and shaved of all head and body hair. Then it is wrapped in a shroud of white cloth and placed in a sitting position with its head bowed on its knees. When an auspicious day has been chosen, the corpse is carried on the back of a special bearer to the sky burial altar. Lamas come from the local monastery to send the spirit on its way and, as they chant the scriptures that release the soul from purgatory, the sky burial master blows a horn, lights the mulberry fire to summon the vultures, and dismembers the body, smashing the bones in an order prescribed by ritual. The body is dismembered in different ways, according to the cause of death, but, whichever way is chosen, the knife work must be flawless, otherwise demons will come to steal the spirit."

A memory of the dissection classes at her university passed before Wen's mind, but she forced herself to continue listening.

"Do the birds ever refuse to eat a body?" she asked.

"Because the vultures prefer eating the flesh to the bones," the sky burial master replied, "we feed the bones to the birds first. Sometimes we mix the smashed bone with yak butter. When somebody has taken a lot of herbal medicine, his body will taste strongly of that medicine and the vultures don't like it. Butter and other additions help make it more palatable. It is essential that the whole body be eaten. Otherwise the corpse will be taken over by demons."

Wen stood and looked at the sky burial site for some time. She heard Tiananmen ask the sky burial master whether it was true that one sky burial master had kept back the heads of all the corpses brought to him and built them into a vast wall of skulls because he had witnessed a murder when he was a child and wanted to keep the ghost of the murderer at bay. She didn't listen to the master's answer. She was trying to reconcile herself to the idea of allowing the sharp, ravenous beak of a vulture to break into the flesh of a loved one. In the time she had been in Tibet, she had grown to understand many of the things that had, at first, horrified and disgusted her. The Buddhist faith was now a part of her life. Why, then, was it so difficult for her to believe, as Zhuoma and Tiananmen did, that sky burial was a natural and sacred rite and not an act of barbarity? If Kejun was the Chinese menba people spoke of, would she be able to bear it?

As they were leaving, she turned to the sky burial master.

"Have you ever performed a sky burial for a Chinese?" she asked.

The master looked at her curiously. "Never," he said. "But Old Hermit Qiangba, who sits beside Lake Zhaling, sings of such a thing."

BACK AT Lake Zhaling, the three friends pitched their tent near the place where Qiangba used to sing so that they could ask the people who came there to collect water whether they knew what had happened to the hermit. Some people told them that Qiangba had walked away over the waves, singing as he went. Others said that his chanting had called the spirits to him and they had summoned him to heaven. But the three of them refused to believe that Qiangba had gone forever, taking their hopes with him.

On the point of despair, they decided to go and make an offering of a mani stone in the hope that it would bring them good fortune. Just as they were making preparations to go, a tall man galloped up to their tent.

"Are you the people looking for Old Hermit Qiangba?"

The three of them nodded in assent, all completely taken aback.

"Then come with me."

Before the words were out, the man had steered his horse back around and whipped it on. With no pause for thought, Wen and the others threw down their bags, jumped onto their horses, and set off in pursuit of the stranger.

Soon they arrived at a tent. They handed their horses' reins to a woman waiting outside and followed the man in. Next to the stove they saw someone sleeping, a thick quilt wrapped around him. Only his pale face was visible.

"Qiangba!" Wen whispered. From the sound of the hermit's breathing, she could tell that his lungs were very weak.

The Tibetan man gestured at them to stay quiet, then took them outside. He guessed from their anxious expressions what it was they were about to ask, and he told them to sit down on the grass.

"Don't worry, I'll explain. One morning a week or so ago, my two daughters came back from fetching water from the lake and said that Old Hermit Qiangba was just sitting there, not singing. My wife thought this unusual and suggested I go and see for myself. So that very day, I rode with my daughters to the lakeside. As they'd said, the hermit was just sitting there in silence, his head bent right over. I walked up to him, shouting his name, but he didn't move or respond in any way. He didn't look well, so I tried shaking him, but he just slumped over. I saw that both of his eyes were screwed shut, and that his forehead and hands were very hot, so I carried him back here on my horse. We have tried giving him some herbal medicine, but it doesn't seem to have had much effect. Although his fever has gone down, he just sleeps all the time and doesn't say anything.

We were thinking of sending him to the monastery nearby to be treated by the lamas.

"Today, when my daughter came back from fetching water, she said she'd heard you'd been staying by the lake for several days, asking after the hermit, so I came looking for you." He glanced inside the tent. "Although everyone around here loves and reveres Old Hermit Qiangba, no one knows where he comes from. All we know is that twenty years ago, he miraculously appeared here and began watching over the lake and singing about King Gesar, Mount Anyemaqen, and our great Tibetan spirits. Sometimes he also sings about how a Chinese menba stopped the fighting between Chinese and Tibetans in this region. People fetching water bring him food, but none of us knows where he lives. Sometimes, people see him talking to lamas from the nearby monastery. Some say that the lamas know all about his past, but I'm not sure. We only come to the Hundred Lakes for the spring and summer."

Although Zhuoma tried to persuade the man that he should allow Wen to take a look at the hermit, the man was adamant that he wished to take him to the nearby monastery. Nor would he allow Zhuoma or Wen to accompany him, since women were not allowed in the monastery and this one had no guesthouse. After a brief discussion, Wen and Zhuoma decided that Tiananmen should go with Qiangba while they would pitch camp nearby and wait for news.

IT WAS many days before Tiananmen returned. Wen could do nothing but wait. She sat in the grass outside the tent and whispered to herself over and over again, "Om mani padme hum." Zhuoma brought her food and helped her lay out her bedding at night. The rest of the time she allowed Wen to remain lost in her thoughts.

When at last Wen saw Tiananmen's horse in the distance, she stood up. He rode straight to her and, without dismounting, passed her a bundle wrapped in yellowing bandages.

"For many years," he said, "Old Hermit Qiangba has kept this safe at the monastery. All he knows about its contents is that they are to be given to a Chinese woman from Suzhou called Shu Wen. He has tried many times to find someone who would take it to Suzhou for him, but no traveler was able to help him. His lungs are a little better now. He has spoken to me about his experiences. I think the package must be for you."

## 8

## THE LOVE OF SKY BURIAL

In the tent, Wen sat transfixed by the bundle. She could almost feel it breathing, waiting to come alive at her command. Finally, with trembling hands, she untied the familiar bandages—the sort used by doctors across China. Inside were two notebooks. Not much was written in either book, but every stroke of every character had been written by the man who had occupied her thoughts day and night for as long as she could remember. Wen's blood was pounding in her veins. After so many years of searching and uncertainty, finally she felt she could see, hear, and feel her husband. Slowly she leafed through the pages, hardly daring to touch them in case they crumbled in her hands. One of the notebooks contained medical notes, recording the ailments that Kejun and his comrades had encountered on entering Tibet and details of their treatment. The other was a diary. On its first page, it said that it was written for Kejun's wife, Shu Wen, for whom Kejun longed with all his heart.

Neither Zhuoma nor Tiananmen knew what to say to Wen, who was trembling and sobbing. No words or gestures could stop the flow of tears that had been accumulating for so long.

Tiananmen lit a lamp and hung it near her. Beside her he placed a flask of oil with which to replenish it. Zhuoma added a few more dung cakes to the fire, then arranged a quilt for Wen by the blaze and guided her over to it. The two of them then silently left the tent.

Wen began reading the diary with great trepidation. In neat handwriting, which grew more erratic over the course of the entries, was recorded the story of what had happened to Kejun.

The first pages were entirely taken up by Kejun's surprise at the resistance his unit was meeting from the Tibetans. During his training he had been led to believe that negotiations between the Chinese government and Tibetan religious leaders had been entirely successful. He had been told that their "warmhearted, honest Tibetan compatriots" welcomed the People's Liberation Army with open arms. His classes on Tibetan customs and government policy toward minorities had done little to prepare him for the aggression he encountered. His unit was composed of young, illiterate peasants whose heads were full of Communist slogans: "Liberate the whole of China!," "On with the Revolution to the end!" They believed that all resistance to them was "counterrevolutionary." Kejun and the unit's commander were the only educated soldiers. Gradually they realized that the Tibetans' hostility stemmed from the fact that they believed the Chinese were unearthly demons sent to destroy their religion. The Tibetans' savagery was legendary: they would not rest until they had torn these demons to pieces. The Chinese soldiers had retaliated.

For weeks Kejun's unit made its way north on horseback, taking great care to skirt areas where Tibetans were living or keeping their flocks. Then one evening as the sun was setting, they heard cries of agony coming from the mountainside. The commander and Kejun—who could both speak a little Tibetan—went on ahead to investigate. As they got closer to the terrible sound, they saw a scene that froze them with horror. A flock of vultures was feeding upon a pile of blood-soaked bodies, one of which was alive and struggling desperately to beat off the birds of prey. Before the commander could stop him, Kejun—with his sense of responsibility toward the sick and injured—whipped out his revolver and shot one of the vultures.

There was a flurry of wings as the birds flew into the air—then an awful silence. The injured man lay twitching on the ground. Kejun was about to walk over to him when a roar of rage cut through the air like a hurricane. He looked up and saw, on the hillside above him, a group of angry Tibetans glaring at him. A shiver ran down his spine. He realized that in his haste to help a dying man, he had intruded on a funeral rite and shot dead a sacred bird. He was terrified to think about the consequences of his rash act—he was also confused as to why no one had been present at the funeral to chant the scriptures, and why a man who was still alive had been left with the corpses.

Keeping a wary eye on the crowd above him, Kejun made his way over to the sky burial site. The man was unconscious. Kejun dressed his wounds and then carried him to his horse. He and the commander rode back to their unit, Kejun holding the injured man in front of him.

The unit tried to keep moving that evening, looking for a suitable place to set up camp, but everywhere they turned, they found the path barricaded by Tibetans, who hurled curses at them. They feared an attack at any moment.

Kejun saw terror in the soldiers' faces. They believed self-sacrifice for the Revolution to be an honor, but they were petrified of Tibetan religious punishments, of which they had heard horrible rumors. Morale was extremely low. They had no water for cooking, few rations, and very little firewood to help them withstand the freezing conditions of a night on the plateau.

It was at this point in the diary that Kejun's handwriting became untidy, as if written in a great hurry. Wen was tempted to read the final entry, so desperate was she to know the truth, but she carried on. She owed it to Kejun to read the whole story.

In his diary, Kejun debated with himself about what to do. The Tibetans clearly would not let them carry on with their journey. They wanted revenge for what Kejun had done. It was only a matter of time before they attacked the unit, and who knows how many soldiers would be massacred. The unit had sent a radio signal to their command post, but had received no reply. There was no certainty that relief would be sent. If they didn't act soon, who knew what would happen.

Kejun felt that since he was the one who had caused this situation, he should go to the Tibetans and explain his actions. Perhaps that way he would win a truce for his comrades. He laid down his pen full of uncertainty about what the next day would hold.

At first light, Kejun went to check on the Tibetan he had rescued from the savage beaks of the vultures. By then he was able to swallow food and tell Kejun his name, Qiangba. With great difficulty, and pausing for breath after every sentence, he told Kejun what had happened.

He was a young lama from a monastery in the north, he explained. He had come to this area with other lamas to gather medicines, but they had encountered fierce fighting between the Tibetans and Chinese. To make matters worse, Qiangba had fallen ill. His lungs had become very weak and he was drifting in and out of consciousness. His companions took him to stay in a nearby monastery, but while they were there, news came that the Chinese army was approaching. In a panic, the lamas forced medicine down Qiangba's throat, hid him on a mountain ridge outside the monastery, and fled.

Qiangba didn't know exactly what happened next but he thought that his apparently lifeless body must have been found by a group of men on their way to perform a sky burial, and added to the corpses. He imagined that the men had fled the sky burial site on hearing of the approach of the Chinese. They had not had time to cover up the corpses, whose shrouds had just been taken off in preparation for dismemberment. Qiangba had regained consciousness just as a massive bird was attacking his chest.

His story told, Qiangba knelt at Kejun's feet and thanked him for saving his life.

Kejun stopped him. "Do you think you can stand?" he asked.

The young lama nodded.

"Then come with me," Kejun said, leading Qiangba to where the commander was eating his meager breakfast. He explained to the commander that Qiangba was willing to take him to find water and asked for permission to leave the unit. Impressed by Kejun's courage, the commander readily agreed.

Kejun then sat down and scribbled the last entry in his diary. At the end of it, he wrote a letter to Wen.

> *My darling Wen,*
>
> *If I don't return today, others will tell you what happened to me. Please understand and forgive me.*
> *I love you. If I am allowed into paradise, I'll make sure you live a safe and peaceful life, and wait for you there. If I go to hell for this, I will give everything I have to pay*

*the debts we both incurred in life, working
to give you the right to enter heaven when
your time comes. If I become a ghost, I'll
watch over you at night and drive away
any spirits that trouble your rest. If I have
no place to go to, I'll dissolve into the air
and be with you at your every breath.
Thank you, my love.*

*Your husband, who thinks of you day and
night,
Kejun
On this day, which both of us will never
forget.*

Wen turned the next page, but the rest of the diary was blank.

She felt the room spin and a dark shadow fall over her. Then she fainted.


WHEN WEN came around it was pitch-dark in the tent except for a small, flickering butter lamp. Tiananmen and Zhuoma were sitting with their prayer wheels, muttering prayers for her. She fell into a deep sleep that seemed as bottomless as Lake Zhaling. In her dreams she heard the wistful singing of Qiangba the hermit.

She didn't know how long she slept, but she awoke to find Zhuoma sitting beside her.

"There is something you should see," Zhuoma said, taking her hand.

Outside the tent, more khata scarves than she could count were fluttering in the breeze and a crowd of people stood waiting for her. In the middle of this crowd, she could see Old Hermit Qiangba sitting on the ground, flanked by two lamas.

"He is not a ghost," said Zhuoma. "He has ridden here from the monastery. He has had a recurring problem with his lungs ever since he was abandoned in the mountains as a young man. But he felt sufficiently recovered to come here to see you. He wanted to meet the wife of the man who saved his life."

The hermit rose shakily to his feet and walked over to Wen. Presenting her with a khata scarf, he bowed deeply.

"Most respected hermit," said Wen. "I have read in my husband's diary that he wanted to explain to the angry men surrounding his unit why he had shot a sacred vulture. He took you with him. Please, can you tell me what happened?"

Qiangba sat down on the grass and signaled to Wen to sit beside him.

"Your husband told me that he knew a way to call

back the sacred vulture that he had killed. He wanted me to take him to the men he had offended so that he could make amends for having disturbed the sky burial. I believed him. I led him to where the men were, up on the mountainside. First I foolishly tried to explain to them what had happened to me, but they wouldn't listen. They looked at me in horror. They thought that I had been transformed into a ghost because demons had interrupted my burial. They believed that because one sacred vulture had been killed, no more vultures would return to earth and the Tibetan people would be consigned to hell. They were about to set upon us with knives when your husband pulled out his gun and fired a shot into the air. There was a momentary stillness and he used the opportunity to shout to the men to let me go.

" 'I beg you to listen,' he said in faltering Tibetan. 'Let this man go to my friends to tell them that I must remain here to put right my insult to the messengers of the spirits. I am going to call back the sacred vulture. Otherwise, none of your vultures will ever return and you will never enter heaven.'

"Reluctantly the men parted to let me through. As I was leaving, your husband passed me a bundle tied up in bandages.

" 'If anything happens to me,' he said, 'make sure my wife receives this.'

"I was still very weak and it was difficult for me to move away quickly. As soon as I was at a safe distance, I stopped to rest behind a thicket. From there I watched your husband lay down his pistol and prostrate himself on the ground. He then knelt before the crowd of men and addressed them. His words drifted over to my hiding place.

" 'Neither I nor the other Chinese have come here to harm you. All we wanted to do was bring Chinese knowledge to you, to improve your lives, as Princess Wencheng did more than a thousand years ago. She taught you how to weave, how to grow crops and treat your illnesses. We wanted to tell you how to use new materials to improve your tents, how to make new sorts of leather goods, how to make your animals grow fatter. We wanted to help you conquer the demons of sickness that cause you pain. Although we carry weapons, we don't want to use them against you. We only use them like you use your knives, to protect ourselves from evil people.

" 'I did what I did yesterday to save one of your lamas, who had not died, as you believed. However, I have realized that I made a mistake in killing one of your sacred messengers. I wish to atone for this mistake. I will sacrifice my own life to call the vultures back. According to your religion, the sacred vultures will not eat a demon. After I die, I ask you to cut my body up with your knives, and see for yourselves whether we Chinese are the same in death as you Tibetans. If the spirits send down their vultures as a sign, please believe that we Chinese see them as our friends also, that hatred and bloodshed are the work of demons, that in the eyes of the spirits we are all brothers!' "

Qiangba looked up at the sky.

"Your husband then picked up his pistol from the ground and, facing toward his home in the east, shot himself through the head."

The hermit paused. Wen, too, gazed at the sky. After a few moments of respectful silence, he continued with his story.

"Overwhelmed by grief, I limped back to the camp to tell the commander what had happened. He rushed to the place I had described, the other soldiers hard on his heels. But it was impossible for him to rescue your husband's body from the vultures. The men had dismembered it with their knives and the earth was covered in hungry birds.

"Perhaps, in the menba's body, they could taste the sincerity of his desire for peace," said Qiangba.

"Perhaps there was something magical in the appearance of so many birds. Whatever the reason, the vultures lingered there for a long time, wheeling and circling the summit of the mountain.

"The soldiers saw the Tibetans watching them respectfully from a distance. By your husband's action, they had realized that the Chinese could also be carried into the sky by the sacred birds. His death had taught them that Chinese flesh and Chinese feelings were identical to theirs. As the soldiers made their way back to the camp, khata scarves lined their path, performing a memorial dance under the blue sky and white clouds.

"The commander continued onward with his troops. I made the journey back to my monastery. Before we parted, the instructor asked if I would take care of Kejun's package and see if I could find an honest traveler who would take it to a woman called Shu Wen in Suzhou. He was worried that he and his men would not return to China alive. I promised him that I would do as he asked. When I returned to the monastery, I beseeched the abbot to allow me to wander the countryside singing of the Chinese menba who had saved my life and washed away the hatred between Tibetans and Chinese with his own. Since that time, no blood has been shed between Tibetans and Chinese in this area. Try as I might, I never found a traveler I trusted to bring you this parcel. Now, instead, you have come to me."

HAVING LISTENED to the hermit's story, Wen prostrated herself before the crowd of onlookers with their fluttering khata scarves, and prayed: "Om mani padme hum."

9

## THE JOURNEY HOME

It was time for Wen to leave the Hundred Lakes, snowcapped Anyemaqen, and the other mountains of Qinghai. For years she had wandered in this region. Its grasslands, waters, and sacred mountains filled her soul. Here she had sampled all the joys and sorrows of human life. Here her love for Kejun had grown in intensity. Here she had found her spiritual home. Though her body was leaving, her spirit would remain in the place that held her dead husband. As she prepared for her journey, her heart was like still water; any ripples of longing or sadness had been gently smoothed away by the influence of the spirits. Wen knew that in the months and years to come, at all times and in all places, she would be like a kite, connected by an invisible thread to Mount Anyemaqen.

She divided in two her book of essays, its pages overwritten with all her words of longing. One half she would carry back with her to China, the other half she would leave with Old Hermit Qiangba. In this way, a part of Kejun and a part of herself would live on in Tibet.

It was decided that Wen, Zhuoma, and Tiananmen should make their way to Lhasa, the most ancient and holy city of Tibet. There they could seek out representatives of the Chinese army to see what was known about Kejun's fate. They could also inquire about transport to China. Zhuoma was determined to make one final journey to Wen's homeland, and Tiananmen wished to see the place that had been Zhuoma's inspiration, before returning to his monastery. One of the families camped by the lake promised that they would seek out Gela's family and take a message to them.

THE JOURNEY south was arduous, their path a lonely one. However, once they had crossed over the Tanggula mountain range, they met many more travelers on their route, which took them into more populated land. To their surprise, they began to notice Chinese faces at the markets and fairs. There were restaurants and shops with signs written in

Chinese characters. Tiananmen was particularly taken aback by what they saw. It was as if they had walked into another world—or century. One day they even found themselves in a village square where young men and women dressed in multicolored combinations of Chinese and Tibetan clothing strutted up and down to music. One of the onlookers told Wen that this was a "fashion show."

Wen had never expected to find so many Chinese settled here, with families and businesses. She had never imagined that all the terror and bloodshed she had witnessed would have resulted in this. So much had been happening while she had been in the wilderness. What did the Chinese settlers make of this mysterious country and its culture? Part of her longed to be able to engage some of these people in conversation. Another part of her held back, remembering how difficult it had been when she had talked to Chinese people at the Dharmaraja festival.

WHAT THEY had seen on their journey was nothing compared to the teeming streets of Lhasa, the huge white Potala Palace looming over them. As the three friends made their way into the city, they felt faint with the hustle and bustle, the unfamiliar noise and smells. Wen was overwhelmed with a huge nostalgia for her homeland. Except for the temples and the people in Tibetan dress, she felt she could almost be back in China, especially in the streets of the Barkhor market district, where Chinese and Tibetan traders jostled with each other to hawk their wares. Tiananmen was utterly bemused by what he saw. He rubbed the back of his head in astonishment. To him the uses of all these exotic objects were a complete mystery. Zhuoma seemed partly dismayed, partly exhilarated by the scene.

"It hardly seems like Tibet," she said.

Tiananmen pointed at a group of lamas at a stall shouting out the religious articles they had for sale—rosaries, prayer flags, jewel-encrusted yak skulls, and goods for offerings.

"What scriptures are they chanting?" he asked. Although Wen and Zhuoma knew the lamas were not praying, they were just as surprised as him to see lamas engaging in trade.

In the market, Zhuoma bartered a necklace of precious beads for a pen for Wen, a new robe for Tiananmen, and a scarf and some ready money for herself. Over the years, Zhuoma's ancestral jewelry had become greatly depleted, but she still owned just enough to allow the three of them to travel to China.

Evening began to draw in and they realized that they needed somewhere to stay. In a little street, they found a small guesthouse owned by a retired Chinese teacher, who showed them where they could keep their horses. He told them he had been sent to Tibet twenty years ago. He had found it very difficult to settle in, but at least there was less class struggle and political study here. Wen pretended to understand what he was talking about, but her tired mind could make no sense of it. What did he mean by "class struggle" and "political study"?

During the night, Wen and Zhuoma heard an urgent knocking at their door. Wen instinctively reached for her half book of essays, and Kejun's photograph and diary, which she had placed under her pillow before going to sleep. When she opened the door, they found Tiananmen standing there in a state of high excitement.

"Come and look," he said. "We are in heaven."

Wen and Zhuoma followed him to his attic room. He stood by the window. Outside, Lhasa was a blaze of electric light.

Wen and Zhuoma looked at each other. They had each passed nights in Nanjing and Beijing. It was hard to imagine what a modern city must look like to someone who had never seen electricity.

In the morning, the owner of the guesthouse told

Wen she could use his bathroom. As she stood beneath the primitive shower—a thin plastic tube that protruded from a tub of water above her head—she was reminded of her luxurious wash at the army base in Zhengzhou all those years ago, at the beginning of her journey to Tibet. What if she had known then that she wouldn't enter a bathroom again until now? Her older self was astonished by the innocence and bravery of her youth.

Zhuoma said she didn't understand these Chinese gadgets, and scrubbed herself down with water from a bowl. Tiananmen declared he could only wash in the river, and there was nothing the two women could do to persuade him otherwise.

Later that morning, they went to worship at the Potala Palace. Wen stood at the foot of the steep, ladderlike steps that led up to the towering palace. It was the most extraordinary building she had ever seen—vast, beautiful, and taller than she could have imagined. In front of her, crowds of people were climbing the stairway to the palace entrance, stopping every three steps to prostrate themselves. Maybe Kejun had always meant to bring her to this place. Perhaps it was preordained that she should travel all the way to Tibet from the Yangtze delta to make this ascent and be received into the religion of the spirits. She began to climb, bowing like the people around her and quietly intoning, "Om mani padme hum."

Once inside the palace, the three friends made their way along dark corridors, first through a magnificent assembly room, then through courtyards and chapels. There were rooms lined with precious books and scrolls, finely embroidered wall hangings, statues of the Buddha draped in beautiful silk brocade cloths and colored scarves, and many shrines. All was aglow with yellow light from the burning yak-butter lamps.

In the so-called White Palace they marveled at the luxury of the Dalai Lama's living quarters. The architecture and furnishings were exquisite. Delicately wrought golden teapots and jade bowls rested on tea tables. Brocade quilts dazzled the eye with their magnificent embroidery. In the Red Palace they saw the spirit towers, encrusted with gold and precious gems, which contained the remains of past Dalai Lamas. There were thousands of rooms. Wen had had no idea that Tibet contained such wealth. Her head was spinning. She paused to catch her breath. Beside her was a wall painting depicting a marriage. She realized that it was the marriage of Songtsen Gampo to Princess Wencheng, for whom the original palace had been built in the seventh century. She thought of Kejun's last words: "All we wanted to do was bring Chinese knowledge to you, to improve your lives, as Princess Wencheng did more than a thousand years ago." While all around her pilgrims chanted the scriptures, she sat and prayed until Zhuoma drew her away.

EVERYONE THEY talked to in Lhasa told them that they would need permission from the personnel department of their "work unit" to go to China. They could travel to Beijing by airplane, but not without written authority to do so. Zhuoma and Tiananmen were bemused by this. What was a "work unit"? Did they have such a thing? When Tiananmen suggested that his monastery might be his work unit, Wen didn't know whether to laugh or cry. She told them that she would appeal to the military headquarters for the necessary travel documents.

It was not difficult to find the headquarters. All the locals seemed to know where it was and they soon found themselves in front of a military compound whose large gate was inscribed with the words TIBET REGION MILITARY DEPARTMENT. As they stood before it, debating about what to do, an armed guard came toward them and asked politely what they wanted.

"I am here to try to trace my missing husband," she said.

Wen watched the guard make several telephone calls inside the compound and, before long, a man appeared who seemed to be an officer. After asking their names and relationship to each other, he took them into a reception room comfortably furnished with sofas and tea tables.

Tiananmen kept very close to Zhuoma and copied everything she did. He sat down gingerly and was clearly amazed at how soft the sofa was. Wen felt as if she had just walked into a Chinese home. She could still remember how comfortable the battered old sofa in her parents' house used to be. As she sipped the green tea that the officer had brought to them, tears of recognition came to her eyes.

Wen told the officer as briefly as she could about herself and her experiences: about Wang Liang at the Zhengzhou military base, the vehicle convoy that had brought her into Tibet, what had happened to her during the intervening years, and the story of Kejun's martyrdom. She told him that she wished to know what records the army held of Kejun's death and whether they knew of his heroism. She said that she would like to return to China.

The officer looked at her in amazement. He

seemed profoundly moved by what she had told him. He would very much like to help her, he said, but he had only arrived in Tibet eight years ago and had no idea how to start making the inquiries she asked for.

Could he, nevertheless, give them a permit to travel to China? Wen asked him. The officer explained that he needed to confirm their story before he could do so, but he would certainly get in touch with headquarters in Beijing and see what he could find out. He warned her not to be too hopeful: during the Cultural Revolution, many files had been lost or burned.

"What do you mean by the 'Cultural Revolution'?" Wen asked, bemused.

The officer looked at her.

"If you can stay a little longer," he said, "I will try to explain to you what has happened in China over the past thirty years."

Wen and Zhuoma listened in bewilderment as the officer talked of the "Famine" in the 1960s, the "Cultural Revolution" in the 1970s, Deng Xiaoping's "Reform and Opening" in the 1980s, and the "current economic reforms." Tiananmen sat cross-legged in a corner, telling his rosary beads and reciting the scriptures.

Wen had to wait several days before she was summoned by letter to return to the military headquarters. This time she alone was allowed to enter the compound, since Tiananmen and Zhuoma were not named in the letter. There she was greeted by the officer she had met before, along with an older man. The older man apologized that her friends had had to be left outside and promised they would be well looked after. He introduced himself as one of the generals in charge of the troops stationed in Lhasa and told Wen that they had checked all the names and the unit number she had given them. Sadly, there were too many people with the name Wang Liang to be able to trace the particular officer she was talking about, especially since many of the records had been lost and information about that time was so unreliable. However, they had been able to verify that there was indeed a unit with the number she had given based in Chengdu. The records stated, though, that all its members had been killed.

At these words, a pain of disappointment stabbed at Wen's heart.

Seeing the sadness in her face, the general tried to comfort her. He assured her they would continue to look for new information and would look as far afield as possible.

"I do not believe that you will lose heart," he said. "No ordinary person could have spent half a lifetime searching for a husband—only true love can produce determination like that." His words brought tears to Wen's eyes. He suggested that Wen and her two friends move to the guesthouse of the military headquarters, which would be more comfortable for them.

Suddenly Wen was overwhelmed by a physical exhaustion unlike any she had known before. She struggled to her feet.

"Are you all right?" the general asked in concern.

"I'm fine, thank you," she replied. "Just so very tired . . ."

"Please believe me," said the general. "I understand your weariness."

THE MILITARY guesthouse was equipped with all manner of strange modern devices. There were television sets, electric kettles, flushing toilets, and hot running water. Tiananmen was particularly unsettled by their surroundings. Wen sensed that, had they not been treated with such great warmth by Chinese and Tibetans alike, he would not have wanted to stay.

In the days that followed, Wen sat and waited for news. In all her years of living with Gela's family and wandering with Zhuoma and Tiananmen she had learned to renounce desire—to let come what would come.

While she waited, Tiananmen talked to the Tibetan soldiers stationed at the headquarters. They regarded him as a walking bible of horsemanship and would come and ask his advice about how to handle their animals. One of them even invited Tiananmen to visit his parents, who lived in Lhasa. That evening, when Tiananmen returned to the strange guesthouse that so bemused him with its televisions and kettles, he told Wen about how the couple he had met spent their day. In the morning they attended to the family shrine, placing fresh yak butter and water on the altar in the courtyard. Then they climbed onto the flat roof of their house, where they burned scented juniper wood, dedicating the smoke to the spirits of the mountains, waters, and home, and asking for protection. After that, they joined their neighbors to walk the "scripture circuits." Residents of Lhasa and pilgrims from all over Tibet would walk these holy routes, telling their rosary beads and praying. The outer circuit took them around the whole city and was walked early in the morning; the inner circuit took the worshippers around the Hall of the Buddha inside Jokhang Temple, another of Lhasa's imposing and sacred buildings. Tiananmen had been told that you could accumulate several times more merit from walking a scripture circuit than from reading the scriptures elsewhere.

During their stay at the guesthouse, Wen had further opportunities to talk to the general about what had happened to her. She was particularly adamant that Zhuoma and Tiananmen should be allowed to travel with her to China. She explained to him that Zhuoma was the head of an important Tibetan family. She showed him some of Zhuoma's family jewelry as proof of her story. The general promised to do what he could to find documentary evidence of Zhuoma's identity. One afternoon, he came to Wen and Zhuoma in a state of excitement, saying that he had found written records of Zhuoma's clan.

"I'm afraid I have some bad news, though," he said hesitantly. "I have been told that their estate burned down many years ago."

Zhuoma didn't explain to him that she had witnessed the burning of her house. Wen looked at her, but said nothing. She knew that Zhuoma's former home had long ceased to exist for her in any meaningful sense.

Two days later, the general came looking for them again. This time his face was wreathed in smiles.

"Someone in Beijing remembers reading a report

that described Kejun's death exactly as you have told it to me," he said, "and one of them recalled that there was mention of a wife who lived in Suzhou. I think this is enough evidence for us to confirm your identity and grant you permission to travel to Beijing. There you can apply for resettlement and an army pension. As for Zhuoma, we have learned that there was indeed a female heir to your clan's estate, and the uniqueness of your jewelry proves that you are her."

Wen and Zhuoma were filled with happiness, as if for the first time in decades they had been told who they really were. But there was still something that troubled Wen.

"If there were records of Kejun's death," she asked, "why then didn't his death notice mention how he had died, or accord him the status of a revolutionary martyr?"

The general looked at her gravely. "I cannot answer that," he said.


WITHIN A week, Wen, Zhuoma, and Tiananmen found themselves on an airplane to Beijing, equipped with all the paperwork they needed. Zhuoma had been given an official letter of introduction that would allow her to find teaching work at the Minorities Institute in Beijing should she wish it. Tiananmen possessed a document which said that he was on an official visit to China and would then return to his monastery.

Wen didn't say a single word during the flight. Before her eyes passed scene after scene of her life in Tibet. The faces of Gela's family filled her mind. She took out Kejun's creased photograph and battered diaries, and poured a silent stream of tears over them. Kejun would never see his wife again, her face now deeply etched with the spirit of Tibet. He would remain forever on the plateau, beneath the blue sky and white clouds.

Her heart was full of trepidation. Would her parents be alive? Where was her sister? Would her family recognize her?

She unfolded the paper crane, kept prisoner for so many years inside her book, and gently smoothed out her sister's letter. Time had erased all trace of the characters. Her half book of essays felt heavy, as if weighted down with the water and soil of the plateau.

Wen was shaken out of her reveries by the voice of a child asking her mother in Chinese, "Mummy, why does that Tibetan lady smell so bad?"

"Shh, don't be rude," her mother said. "Chinese and Tibetans have very different ways of life. You shouldn't say thoughtless things like that."

Wen looked down at her threadbare and faded clothes. If she was no longer Chinese, who was she? But perhaps that question did not matter. What was important was that her soul had been born. Wang Liang had been right: just staying alive was a victory.

THERE COULD be no comparison between Wen's first-class sleeper compartment on the journey from Beijing to Suzhou and the stuffy sardine can of a train that had carried her to Chengdu all those years ago. It was like the difference between heaven and hell, not to be mentioned in the same breath. In contrast to the Tibetan plateau, the scenes that flew past her window were full of life. She sat and watched the red-brick and gray-tiled houses of Beijing give way to the familiar white houses of the Yangtze delta.

Zhuoma and Tiananmen had not accompanied Wen on her return to Suzhou. She had asked them to wait for her in Beijing. She wished to see her family alone.

Throughout the journey, Wen's tears fell in a

constant stream over her robe. Whenever the train guards or her fellow passengers asked what was wrong, she just shook her head. So concerned was one of the guards that he made a request on the train's loudspeaker for someone who knew sign language or Tibetan to come forward and help.

When the train pulled into Suzhou, the station bore no relation to Wen's memory of it. She assumed it was a new station and began asking directions to Suzhou's old train station. It had been pulled down, she was told. She hailed a taxi, but the driver hadn't heard of the place she wanted. After much discussion, he worked out that she was referring to a street in the suburbs that had been demolished ten years ago. He kept looking at her as if she were some kind of monster and she had to plead with him to drive her there.

When they arrived, she was stunned by the scene that greeted her.

Her sister's courtyard home with its moon gates and the beautiful little garden by the river had disappeared, replaced by row upon row of high-rise buildings. She stood there, dazed, not knowing what to do or whom to ask for help. She approached some construction workers mending a road, but couldn't understand a word any of them said. She finally worked out that they were from the south of Anhui Province and had no idea what had happened in Suzhou in the last three decades. Wen felt utterly lost.

As evening drew in, Wen gathered herself together and found a hotel not far from where her sister's house used to be. A sign with two small stars on it hung above the reception desk, although Wen didn't have a clue as to what that meant. At the desk, she was asked for her identity card but had no idea what that was. Instead, she produced the letter of introduction the Tibetan Military Department had given her. Unwilling to make a decision on her own about whether to let Wen register, the hotel receptionist asked her to wait a moment and disappeared. When she finally returned, she told Wen that she could have a room, but she should go and register at the police station as well.


THAT NIGHT, Wen dreamed she had returned to Tibet with Kejun to look for her parents and sister on the holy mountains. She was woken before daybreak by the roar of traffic. She sat watching it from her window until she fell into a daze. Her eyes were used to the endlessly rolling grasslands. Everything here seemed so crowded that she could make nothing of it. The hometown she had dreamed of had vanished without a trace.

At that moment, she heard the rattle of bamboo clappers below her window. Her heart leaped at the memories the sound awakened: when she was a little girl in Nanjing, the itinerant rice sellers carried such clappers and, when they passed her house, her mother would always buy her a little bowl of sweet fermented rice. Wen rushed out of her room, toward the sound. Outside she saw a familiar sight: a rice seller carrying two buckets suspended from a long pole on his shoulders. In one of the buckets the hot water used to cook the food steamed, heated by a small charcoal-burning stove built in beneath; from the other rose the old intoxicating aroma of fermented rice. Nothing had changed: even the waistcoat the man wore was the same as she remembered.

Wen hurried over to the peddler. He stopped banging his clappers.

"Eat here or take away?" he asked.

"Here," she replied.

She watched him deftly pour a ladle of boiling water into a bowl, then scoop out two lumps of fermented rice with a bamboo spatula.

"Do you want egg?" he asked her. "A sprinkle of osmanthus flowers? How much sugar?"

"Everything, please, and one spoonful of sugar," Wen replied. As he handed her the bowl, she burst into tears.

"Family problems?" the peddler asked her. "Don't be sad. Just take life a day at a time, and the days will pass quickly enough."

Drinking the sweet rice soup, now mixed with her tears, Wen struggled to compose herself.

"How long have you lived here?" she asked in a trembling voice.

"I came here ten years ago," the peddler said. "I was no good for anything else so it was the bamboo clappers for me. But it's not bad work and every day there's something new. Even the road I walk down is different every year."

Wen asked him if he knew her sister and her parents and described to him the house they used to live in. The peddler gave it some thought.

"I'm afraid not," he said. "In the ten years I've lived here, this area has been knocked down and rebuilt three times. The first time was during the 'Three Constructions,' or whatever it was. Then they built a road and a bridge, only to pull them down again. After that they sold a big chunk of land to Singapore. Many people have come and gone around here. These days you hear fewer and fewer local accents."

He went back to banging his clappers.

Wen stood in the middle of the street, paralyzed by the strangeness of her hometown. She was so absorbed in thought that she heard neither the sound of the clappers nor the noise of the cars and bicycles rushing past her only inches away. All she had now were her memories. Would she have the courage to embark on a second search so late in her life? If not, where should she go?

She put her hand into the pocket of her robe where she kept the photograph of Kejun. Laying her fingers on the image that had shared the sweetness, the bitterness, and the sweeping changes of her life for so many years, she whispered, "Om mani padme hum."

Up above, a family of geese flew toward home.

Here, there were neither sacred vultures nor sky burials.

## A LETTER TO SHU WEN

*Most respected Shu Wen,*

*Where are you?*

*For ten years this book has been in my heart, maturing like wine. Now, at last, I can present it to you.*

*I hope that, sometime, you will be able to hear the gasps of admiration that the beauty of your story inspires.*

*I hope that, sometime, you will be able to answer the countless questions that I have for you. At the very least, I would like to know what has become of Zhuoma and Tiananmen, of Saierbao and her family.*

*I have spent many years searching for you, hoping that we might sit together again in the tea-scented Yangtze delta so that you can tell me the story of your life after Sky Burial.*

*Dear Shu Wen, if you see this book and this letter, I earnestly beg you to contact me through my publisher as soon as possible.*

*Xinran*
*London, 2004*

*ACKNOWLEDGMENTS*

*Sky Burial* is the result of years spent learning how to understand and feel Shu Wen's love, the spiritual life of Tibetans, and how different culture, time, life, and death can be for different people.

I don't know how to thank the following people enough: Julia Lovell (who carried a "football player" in her body) and Esther Tyldesley, whose translation allowed *Sky Burial* to be read in English; my editor at Chatto & Windus for helping this book find its readers; Mr. Hao-chong Liu, who spent months helping me with my research and fact-checking in China; Toby Eady, my "bossy" husband with his professional mind and lover's heart; and Random House, booksellers, and you.

I cannot say thanks enough to you who have taken the time to read my books with your interest in and love of China and Chinese women. I have received responses to *The Good Women of China* from all over the world, so full of open hearts and personal memories that I should now have a book called *The Good Women of the World*.

No one likes crying, but tears water our souls. So perhaps my thanks should be to allow you to cry for the Chinese women in my books . . .

Xinran was born in Beijing in 1958 and was a successful journalist and radio presenter in China. In 1997 she moved to London, where she began work on her seminal book about Chinese women's lives, *The Good Women of China*, which has become an international bestseller. *Sky Burial* is her second book.

The text of this book is set in Minion, a font created in 1990 for Adobe Systems. Type designer Robert Slimbach drew his inspiration from the elegant, readable types of the late Renaissance, combining beauty with functionality to create a font that is suitable for many uses.